FRAME GAMES

The Instructional Design Library
Volume 24

FRAME GAMES

Harold D. Stolovitch
Universite de Montreal

and

Sivasailam Thiagarajan
Instructional Alternatives
Bloomington, Indiana

Danny G. Langdon
Series Editor

Educational Technology Publications
Englewood Cliffs, New Jersey 07632

Library of Congress Cataloging in Publication Data

Stolovitch, Harold D
  Frame games.

  (The Instructional design library; v. 24)
  Bibliography: p.
  1. Educational games. I. Thiagarajan, Sivasailam,
joint author. II. Title. III. Series: Instructional
design library; v. 24.
  LB1029.G3S76   371.3   79-26476
  ISBN 0-87778-144-3

Printed in the United States of America.

Library of Congress Catalog Card Number:
79-26476.

International Standard Book Number:
0-87778-144-3.

First Printing: March, 1980.

To

Serge Berthelot

Daniel Dupont

Andre Hubert

Louise Sauve

for whom all learning is a game

FOREWORD

As a designer of instructional designs, I have admired those of my colleagues who look around themselves for existing "systems" which can be readily transposed to instructional applications. Stolovitch and Thiagarajan seem to have a particular knack for doing just this. They delve into their own experiences and those of others to find that with which we are familiar and take advantage of it. Their skill in doing so is well demonstrated in this book on the subject of "Frame Games."

All of us have played familiar (seemingly, children's) games, such as Tic-Tac-Toe, Bingo, and a variety of card games. But, did you ever think of how these games can be extended to assist in both simple and complex learning needs? Are there learning outcomes to be derived from these games other than the fun, enjoyment, and logic which they demand and give? You may be very surprised to find out that there are many varied outcomes beyond simply having fun. To realize what these other uses and benefits are for learning, we will need to learn how these games (really the "play" of each) can be translated into our students' learning needs. This book will describe and illustrate exactly how the translation can be accomplished. The readers should have little difficulty in seeing how these games, and others, can be used for students.

Danny G. Langdon
Series Editor

PREFACE

The term "frame game" may not be very prevalent, but the concept which it stands for is in common use. Many teachers and trainers have used the structure of some popular game to organize and present different content to help learners achieve different instructional objectives. In this book, we have attempted to describe a systematic procedure for using time-tested game frames to present various instructional content. We have illustrated this procedure with a number of examples from various subject-matter areas and grade levels.

Most instructional design formats require the designer to create both the content and the process for learning; in the frame game approach, a standard process is provided to the designer for loading the new content. The use of frame games drastically cuts down the time required for developing effective instruction. This efficiency gives frame games their versatility—and the designer, a dangerous temptation. It is easy to abuse a single, simple frame game to teach all things to all learners.

We have attempted to reduce this dangerous temptation by providing a variety of examples of frame games and by insisting that you check the appropriateness of this approach to achieve your instructional objectives. In addition to the examples of different frame games and frame variations, we emphasize the process of discovering new frame games from different sources, analyzing their structures, unloading the old content, and loading the new.

We are indebted to the hundreds of participants in our frame game workshops for providing the examples used in this book. We hope that you will be able to use them as models in creating your own unique variations.

H.D.S.
S.T.

CONTENTS

ABSTRACT

FRAME GAMES

Frame games provide a useful tool for efficient, interactive instruction. Like any other game, a frame game represents a "contrived" situation with some elements of conflict and rules for the control of moves and the termination of the game. In addition, the frame game has the unique characteristic of changeable content. By permitting replacement of the old content with some new one, frame games permit rapid redesign of the instructional activity to accommodate a variety of players and to help them achieve instructional objectives at varying levels of complexity.

Frame games may be analyzed in terms of their structure and content, and in terms of rules, player roles, background scenarios, and scoring systems. Both already existing classic recreational games and newly designed content-free frame games are available. Although the reloaded games direct attention away from the teacher or trainer, these game leaders play a key role in conducting the game in such a way as to maximize its effects. If the play of a frame game is not carefully monitored, the result may be unexpected and undesirable.

The procedure for creating an instructional game through the frame game approach begins with the specification of the instructional purpose and the key elements to be incorporated in the game. Then, a suitable frame is selected and an adapted version is produced. This version is revised on the basis of inputs from experts and feedback from actual tryouts with representative players.

FRAME GAMES

I.

USE

"Let's play a game! Yesterday you learned about some of the tools we use in a woodwork shop. You saw a set of slides on how each tool has its own special job to do. You visited Mr. Schreiner's shop, saw him working with his tools, and even had a chance to handle some of them. Today, I've got a game for us to play. It's called TOOL BOX.

"Here is a card for each of you. Each card has five rows of picture names of tools. There are five pictures in each row. Every card has different pictures in different places, but in the middle of all the cards is a free tool box. (See Figure 1.) With one of the wooden chips I've given you, you may cover the free tool box right now. Good. Now I'm going to draw names of tools from this bag. If you see that tool on your card, cover it with a wooden chip. The first one to cover five tools in a line either up and down, sideways, or from corner to corner should shout "TOOL BOX!" I'll check his or her card to see if he or she is right. (See Figure 2.) The winner gets to call out the next set of tool names . . ."

You have just had an opportunity to hear the introduction to an instructional game for sixth-grade children who are being initiated into a six-week module on woodworking. Perhaps you noticed that the game bore a strong resemblance to the popular game of BINGO. That is not surprising since the teacher designed his game using the frame game ap-

Figure 1

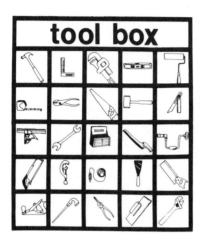
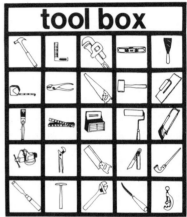

Figure 2

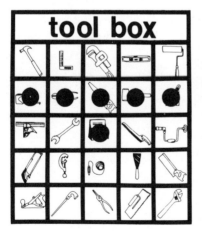
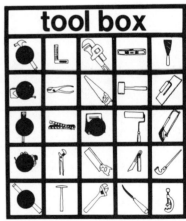

proach, which is essentially a design technique that adapts old games to meet new instructional objectives. That is what this book is about: the frame game approach to creating new and exciting games from time-tested game frameworks.

Why Use Instructional Games?

Even though we wish it were otherwise, the majority of educational activities still center around teacher presentations plus textbook. The entire *Instructional Design Library* (of which this volume is a part) presents a broad range of alternative approaches in an attempt to break this virtual monopoly within the teaching-learning process. Instructional games represent perhaps the most motivating of all these designs. The ever-increasing array of games on the market attests to an accelerating interest in them. Games exist in virtually every culture. Anthropologists and sociologists point to the vital role games and play activities occupy in every society. Through the use of games, children acquire social skills, model their future adult roles, and become enculturated into their community.

Games have been used for instructional purposes within the classroom for centuries because they make learning an enjoyable activity. "Let's play a game!" almost always elicits positive responses even from the least motivated learner.

With the increasing emphasis on individualization in both education and training comes the specter of solitary confinement and isolation. Instructional games offer learners the chance of getting together to learn—at any age level. The DIFFUSION GAME by Michael Molenda is an adult-level game in which prospective change agents compete against the conservative influences of an educational institution as they try to introduce innovations within a specified period of time. In another example, fourth-graders learn to multiply and divide through a children's game called TRAIN where the object is to move more spaces during each round than in the previous one. Here, players attempt to surpass *their own standards*. Although these two games are different from each other, they have their antecedents in older games.

Instructional frame games can not only be used at any level but also with any type of student. Let us take TIC-TAC-TOE as an example. Its basic framework can be adapted to provide an initial consonant game for second graders or a game about prospective medicine for mature adults. The TOOL BOX game described in the opening paragraphs of this chapter could be modified for junior high school. SLAPJACK is a simple children's game in which players turn over cards, slapping only the jacks in the deck. This frame game has been adapted and modified to encompass all levels of learners from pre-schoolers dealing with recognition of different geometric shapes to sophisticated students of veterinary medicine grappling with the identification of various bovine respiratory ailments.

In addition to their application with a broad range of learners, instructional frame games encompass all types of subject matter. Usually, games used for education or training deal with cognitive objectives. CONCENTRATION type games, where students match capitals with countries or chemical elements with their symbols, or race board games, where students answer a question to progress around a track, are the most usual varieties. At a more complex cognitive level, executive decision-making games and problem-solving games are growing in popularity. A number of teachers who are concerned with the attainment of affective objectives have also turned to instructional frame games as a tool for attitude change. The GREAT DEBATE game is an example of such a frame game which has been used to explore attitudes on topics ranging from abortion to zoning laws. With pre-schoolers and handicapped learners, instructional frame games have been found highly useful for acquiring psychomotor manipulative skills. Games of this nature range from the simple type where learners fill holes with appropriately shaped counters to those requiring complex performances to operate prosthetic devices.

Limitations of Instructional Games

Instructional frame games help teachers and instructors design motivating materials to meet a wide variety of objectives. Yes, games are fun, but they have to be used with caution. As with other group-participation activities, games tempt the strong to dominate the others. Unless carefully monitored, one or two aggressive players can quickly take over the game, causing other players to withdraw. Competition can also become fierce sometimes during the play of a game. Winning the game may become far more important than the instructional objectives.

Games are also hard acts to follow. Particularly with younger children, playing games is so exciting an activity that the next lesson which requires less intense participation pales by comparison with the preceding game. The timing of the game, the monitoring of its play, and the termination and transition to less motivating learning activities are all important factors that must be taken into consideration whenever games are used in instruction.

Summary

Games represent an instructional design format which is a flexible tool in any instructional designer's repertoire. By utilizing the frame game approach, teachers and trainers can design and develop instructional games which motivate learners and foster collaborative action at any learning level and in virtually all subject-matter areas. Instructional frame games can be applied to help learners achieve cognitive, affective, and psychomotor objectives. However, there are some dangers and limitations to their use, including the possibility of encouraging domination by aggressive people and a withdrawal by their peers, an overemphasis on competition to the detriment of learning, and an excess of excitement which makes them difficult acts to follow.

II.

OPERATIONAL DESCRIPTION

Having discussed some of the uses and dangers of instructional frame games, let us now attempt an analysis of this instructional design format.

Critical Characteristics of Instructional Frame Games

As with all games, instructional frame games contain elements of conflict, control, closure, and contrivance.

When people think of conflict in games, their immediate thought is that of players being pitted against one another. It is true that competition is often a significant factor in most games, including our sample TOOL BOX game. Failure to recognize a particular tool can result in players losing the game. After several rounds, however, the inter-player conflict begins to diminish as chance assumes greater and greater importance. Players now work against "the luck of the draw" as they become more familiar with the tool names.

Conflict. Conflict in games need not always have to take the form of competition among individual players. Some instructional frame games utilize time limits as a form of conflict. We are most familiar with this type of conflict in the BEAT THE CLOCK type of game. To impress on students the proper uses of tools, a game called FIX-IT-FAST was devised by our instructor. In this game, players randomly draw a specified number of cards from a deck labeled "repair

9

situations." A number of other cards containing pictures of tools are placed face down on the table. Each player has 60 seconds to turn over the cards and match tools with repair situations. All players compete against time. In this game, there can be any number of winners as long as players complete the task before the 60 seconds are up.

Other approaches to conflict in instructional frame games may include competition between teams as in any other team game. A special type of competition or conflict is against the game designer or manager. Molenda's DIFFUSION GAME provides an excellent example of this type of conflict. Players have a specific number of months (represented by number of turns), to introduce an innovation in a school. Success depends on discovering the combination of moves and the optimum strategy which is needed to bring about the acceptance of the innovation. The game designer has built in a model of change-agent strategies and their probable outcomes into the rules of the game. The conflict is between the players and the model, which only the game designer and game manager know. The model represents basic principles of diffusion of innovations; hence, the conflict in this game reflects the real-world conflicts due to resistance toward change.

Control. All instructional frame games have rules to control players' behavior. These may be either simple, as in the case of SLAPJACK, where all that is required is to turn over cards and slap the jacks, or highly complex, as in the case of sophisticated computer simulation games, such as COMMERCIAL CREDIT SIMULATION, which involves a number of interrelated rules from various sources reflecting governmental and industrial regulations. Game rules may also be either explicit or implicit. In the game of TOOL BOX, players are told how, where, and when to place their chips to cover squares. These are examples of explicit rules. Such rules as the player covering squares only on his or her own card or the players not changing cards with each other in the middle of the game are not explicitly expressed, but are clearly understood by all the players.

Closure. Instructional frame games provide means for terminating play. Some games, like TIC-TAC-TOE, require only a few minutes to end. Others, like SIMSOC, an economics simulation game, may last an entire semester. Games may be brought to a conclusion by a time limit (as in GOT-A-MINUTE), a criterion score (as in CRIBBAGE), or elimination (as in SPELLING BEE). Winners may be determined by a single win criterion, such as the checkmate in CHESS, or on the basis of multiple criteria, as in the STEEP game, where winners are determined in various categories depending on efficiency, accuracy, and development of positive-attitude-toward-the-instructional-material scores. Instructional frame games may have single winners, as in the game of CLUE, or multiple winners, as in the DIFFUSION GAME, where every player who gets the innovation adopted (within the constraints of the game) wins.

Contrivance. Instructional frame games are not reality; they are contrived activities. Some of the games contain no reflection of reality. These are non-simulation games. BINGO is an example of a non-simulation instructional frame game. At the other extreme are such high-fidelity simulation games as war games in which real tanks and soldiers are used, people are captured, and the winner is the team that actually takes a given territory. Between these two extremes lies a broad spectrum of lower level simulation games including such favorites as MONOPOLY, CHESS, and STOCK MARKET. In all cases, players participate in contrived activity into which they enter from (and from which they can return to) the day-to-day real world. No matter how seriously one plays the game STOCK MARKET, all one ever wins or loses is play money.

Two additional critical characteristics distinguish instructional frame games from other types of games: *learning objectives* and *changeability.*

Learning objectives. Games are usually played for the fun of it. Instructional games, in contrast to recreational games, have a learning purpose behind them. This is best illustrated by comparing the games of BINGO and TOOL BOX:

	BINGO	TOOL BOX
1. *Materials*	5x5 grids with a free square in the center. Chips to cover squares.	5x5 grids with a free square in the center. Chips to cover squares.
2. *Rules*	Numbers are called out. Players cover appropriate squares. Winner is the first to get five squares covered horizontally, vertically, or diagonally.	Tools are called out. Players cover appropriate squares. Winner is the first to get five squares covered horizontally, vertically, or diagonally.
3. *Number of players*	Any number can play.	Any number can play.
4. *Time required*	Approximately five minutes.	Approximately five minutes.
5. *Skills required*	Aural-visual discrimination and association.	Aural-visual discrimination and association.
6. *Objective*	Recreational.	Players will be able to associate names of tools with their appearance.

As can be readily seen from this comparison, the principal difference between the game lies in the purpose of each. TOOL BOX is an instructional game—one of many that could be developed from the recreational game of BINGO. The objective for TOOL BOX involves a fairly straightforward, multiple discrimination task. Objectives for other instructional game adaptations of the BINGO frame game can be at different levels of complexity. BINGO is thus both a recreational game in and of itself and an instructional frame game by virtue of its capacity to generate other games that help players learn.

Changeability. Leaving the most unique characteristic for last, we come to an attribute that distinguishes an instructional *frame game* from an ordinary instructional game. The characteristic of changeability endows frame games with the chameleon-like quality of being able to be adapted to accommodate a wide variety of instructional content and objectives. TOOL BOX and a whole host of other instructional games have been designed using the basic BINGO framework. The ease with which BINGO allows its original content to be unloaded (i.e., the five categories of numbers) and then reloaded with different types of new content, makes BINGO stand out as an excellent example of a frame game.

Combining the critical characteristics described above, we can define an instructional frame game *as a design that provides a framework for creating contrived learning activities involving conflict, a set of rules for player moves, and termination criteria so that winners may be determined. This framework is easily adaptable to a wide variety of instructional objectives and content.*

Variable Characteristics of Instructional Frame Games

The critical characteristics of conflict, control, closure, contrivance, learning objectives, and changeability are essential requirements of instructional frame games. In addition, instructional frame games also have a number of variable characteristics. These include the level of complexity of the learning objectives, the types and numbers of players, the media, and the source of frame games.

Level of complexity. Instructional frame games can be used to meet a wide variety of objectives from simple recall to highly complex problem-solving. The TOOL BOX game is an example of a frame game with a fairly simple instructional objective. In contrast, an adaptation of the basic SNAKES AND LADDERS framework, called DRIVING TEST, which helps players learn about driving a car, possesses more complex transfer and application objectives. This game has players move from square to square along a road toward the goal of obtaining their driver's license. Each square requires the driver to make the next move in a complex situation. Various stimuli, such as meshing gear noises, racing engines, or erratic behaviors of approaching cars, are presented on cards placed at different points along the board. The driver is forced to decide how he or she must respond to each situation. Errors result in breakdowns, stalls, or even accidents. Other chance elements, such as detours, heavy traffic, and one-way streets, can send the player-driver back down the board.

NAKED MONSTERS is a series of concept-learning games for teacher training. Such frame games as SLAPJACK and WAR provide the framework for NAKED MONSTER games, which deal with the training objectives of performing a concept analysis and selecting divergent examples and close-in nonexamples for teaching and testing. At the rule-using level, a frame game called EMERGENCY has been used to help warehouse employees make decisions on the best procedures to follow in emergency situations.

Instructional frame games can be utilized for problem-solving goals. The CONFRONTATION game pits people in conflict against one another while a mediating party attempts to achieve agreement between opposing camps before time runs out and everyone loses. This game requires that individuals with opposing interests solve their problems in the face of external pressures. Mediators have to bring opposing forces together. Each player has a different scoring system: For the conflicting parties, the more they give up, the more they lose, yet, if they do not give up enough, they lose the game. For the mediators, the score is based on the opponents' compromises. This game has been used to provide problem-solving opportunities for such diverse groups as campus ministers, feminist militants, and institutionalized juvenile delinquents.

These few examples illustrate the various ways in which instructional frame games can be employed to meet learning objectives at different levels of complexity.

Types and numbers of players. Just as instructional frame games can be adapted to meet different objectives, they can also be used with a broad variety of learners and sizes of groups. To illustrate, let us take the basic TIC-TAC-TOE game and expand the grid from three-by-three to four-by-four in size.

THIS WILL KILL YOU is a consumer health game for adults. The game is designed to assist players in identifying high probability killers for various age, race, and sex groups. The expanded TIC-TAC-TOE grid used in this game looks like the one shown in Figure 3. Three "X's" or "O's" in a line (as in TIC-TAC-TOE) win. This particular game involves teams and a judge. While the teams compete, the remaining class members, like the audience in a TV game, participate vicariously.

The same basic frame game has been adapted for a junior high school French class with infinitives across the top and verb forms along the side. The game grids are printed on pads. An answer booklet is supplied to the player who has the turn for being the judge. Three students at a time are

Figure 3

"THIS WILL KILL YOU"

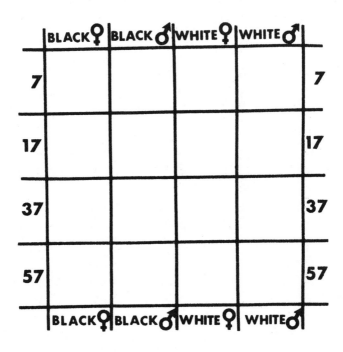

involved in this game. Another adaptation of the same game for elementary school math involves only two players, who are required to multiply the column and row numbers to occupy any cell in the grid (see Figure 4).

The Design Format chapter of this book presents a series of games which handle as many as 100 players with diverse backgrounds and capabilities.

Media. Frame games do not restrict themselves to any specific media format. The same basic frame can generate a host of divergent media adaptations. The table below shows

Figure 4

Grid for MULTIPLY

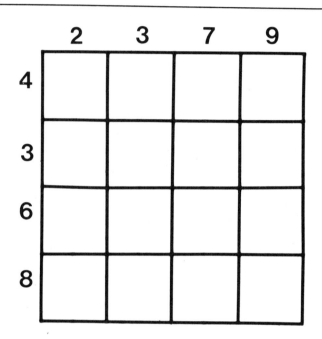

how different participants in a recent game-design workshop altered the media format of the simple frame of SLAPJACK to accommodate a variety of instructional objectives:

Adaptation	Media Format
SHAPES (Elementary Geometry.)	Index cards with teacher-made pictures of different shapes. This card game is played by small groups of five or six players.

FOTO FLASH (Over- and under-exposure in outdoor photography.)	Slides illustrating different levels of over- and under-exposure are projected on a screen. Individual players have three cards with the labels "over," "under," and "correct." First player to hold up the card with the correct label wins the round. The game is played with large groups of ten to 30 players.
CLOUDS (Recognition of different types of clouds.)	Large photographic posters showing different types of clouds. These posters are held up one at a time by the instructor. First player in a medium-sized group of six to eight players who shouts out the correct label for the type of cloud wins that round.
DISRUPTION (Recognition and correct classification of disruptive behaviors in the classroom.)	A videotape cassette is played on a recorder which is linked to a microcomputer. In this computer-assisted solitaire game, the player has a touch-tone "button box." Any time the player sees a disruptive behavior portrayed in the videotape segment, he or she is to press the correct numerical classification code.

Source of frame games. To say that there is nothing new under the sun is somewhat trite. Nevertheless, most modern games are adaptations of earlier ones, having evolved until they are able to stand as unique in their own right. We can divide up frame games, for purposes of convenience, into two major sub-groups: (1) those which already exist as popular, recreational games with given content which can be readily unloaded; and (2) those which have been deliberately designed as frame games and have no original content of their own. Both types can be used in a broad range of instructional situations.

Summary

Instructional frame games possess the four classic attributes of a game—conflict, control, closure, contrivance—as well as the special characteristics of learning objectives and changeability. Instructional frame games may be used at varying levels of complexity to accommodate a variety of player types and group sizes, using different media. Frame games may have already existed as classic games for ages or have been specifically created recently.

III.

DESIGN FORMAT

Designing games is not something that can be done mechanically by following a clearly defined set of rules. This is also true of designing frame games. A "frame game" is not so much a type of game as it is an attitude toward gaming. Developing the "frame game attitude" is essential, then, to the design process. That is the focus of this chapter. Coming up with imaginative and playable games from suggested frames requires you to participate in a half-play, half-design role from the start. Frame gaming forces the designer to test his or her own product, often in a learner role.

Structure and Content

An instructional game may be divided into two basic parts: structure and content. The structure is the way in which a game is put together. The various phases of the game, the moves, the way in which players relate to each other, the element of chance, the rule for winning, the number of players, and the types of strategies necessary to successfully play are all part of the structure. The content relates specifically to the game's learning material and the instructional objectives placed within this structure. A well-designed instructional game is one in which structure and content have been harmoniously matched.

Flexibility is necessary to match structure and content.

Referring back to our emphasis on frame gaming being an attitude as opposed to straight rule application, the game designer must be prepared to make adjustments to get content and structure to fit together. How is this done?

The matrix in Figure 5 shows the extent to which the content and the structure of a frame game may be changed.

Figure 5

Frame Game Matrix

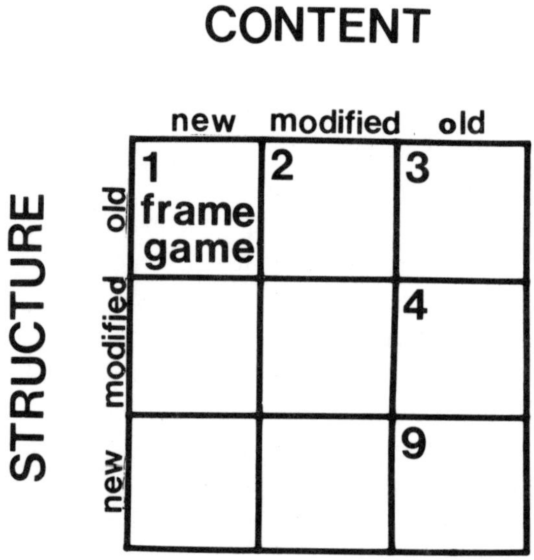

CONTENT

	new	modified	old
old	1 frame game	2	3
modified			4
new			9

(**STRUCTURE** labels the vertical axis)

Cell 1 is our original frame game—for example, BINGO. If we decide to use this game with young children, we may want to reduce the range of possible BINGO numbers, and even use dots instead of numerals. We may also use color clues. Such modifications to the content moves the game to

Cell 2. In the TOOL BOX game, the content has been totally altered. The numbers have been entirely replaced by woodworking tools. Free space is now a free tool box. This pushes the version of the game to Cell 3. However, the game designer has not stopped there. Because of the nature of the woodworking content and learners, he has also been forced to modify the structure somewhat. The label B - I - N - G - O has been removed. Tool names have been placed on the slips which are drawn, and pictures of tools appear on the playing cards. These minor modifications to the structure were necessary to accommodate the new content and learner group. The current version of the game goes to Cell 4 (new content, modified structure).

In the beginning, most designers end up producing instructional games in Cell 4: new content with a slightly modified structure. With practice, however, the designer becomes bolder and ventures farther afield from the original frame, arriving at exciting new structures and content, thus, ultimately creating new games which move him or her to Cell 9.

The Elements of a Frame Game

A convenient way of breaking a frame game (or any game, for that matter) into its component parts is to speak of the rules, roles, scenarios, scoring systems, and media.

Rules. The way in which a game is played is structured by the playing rules. These rules tell the players what may or may not be done. Generally, the rules are explicitly stated at the beginning of the game and are precisely listed in a form which can be referred to during play. Most classic frames generally have simple rules.

In creating a new game from an existing frame game, the rules are generally left more or less intact except for minor modifications to accommodate the needs of new content. TOOL BOX illustrates how the BINGO rules have been modified to meet the requirements of a new content.

Rules for BINGO	Rules for TOOL BOX
To start:	To start:
1. Each player receives a separate BINGO card and a pile of counters.	1. Each player receives a separate TOOL BOX card and pile of wooden chips.
2. Players may cover the center free square with a counter.	2. Players may cover the center free TOOL BOX square with a chip.
Play of the Game:	Play of the Game:
3. A caller randomly pulls numbers, one at a time, from a hat and calls them out clearly. He or she places these on a master sheet, sequentially numbered: B1–B15, I16–I30, N31–N45, G46–G60, O61–O75.	3. A caller randomly pulls cards with names of tools written on them, one at a time from a hat, and calls them out clearly. He or she places these face up in front of him or her.
4. Players cover the numbers as they are called on their playing cards.	4. Players cover the pictures of tools as they are called on their playing cards.
Termination:	Termination:
5. When a player has covered five numbers in a row, either vertically, horizontally, or diagonally, he or she shouts "BINGO."	5. When a player has covered five pictures in a row, either vertically, horizontally, or diagonally, he or she shouts "TOOL BOX."
6. The caller checks the card against the master list of called numbers. If no errors have been made, the player who called "BINGO" is declared the winner.	6. The caller checks the card against the tool cards in front of him or her. If there are no errors, the player who called "TOOL BOX" is declared the winner and becomes the caller for the next round.

Roles. Roles represent the type of characters players assume during the game. Depending on the type of adapted game, roles can either remain very similar to those of the original frame game or differ very markedly. It is safe to say that the more a game contains elements of simulation, the more roles must be altered. To illustrate the degree of change that can occur in roles when creating instructional games from frame games, let us use two examples: one is a non-simulation game and the other involves a high degree of simulation.

Non-simulation frame game: SLAPJACK
Role: Players are themselves. They watch for discarded jacks from an ordinary deck of cards and try to be the first one to slap them.

- -

Adapted game 1: SHAPES
Role: Players are themselves. They attempt to slap a specific shape (e.g., triangle or pentagon) as cards are turned face up.

- -

Adapted game 2: MONSTER MASSACRE
Role: Monster mashers. Teacher-trainee-players slap cards with pictures of monsters containing specific attributes (e.g., trumpet nose and eight arms). Game focuses on concept formation and critical attributes.

Simulation frame game: IDIOTS (Instructional Development in Ordinary Teaching Situations)
Roles: An instructional developer and a subject-matter expert ironing out potential sources of conflict in an instructional development project.

- -

Adapted game 1: CONFRONTATION
Roles: Two parties in conflict on a university campus (e.g., unmarried pregnant coed and conservative father) and a mediator (e.g., campus minister).

Adapted game 2: BARGAINING TABLE
Roles: Management representatives and labor delegates in a dispute over a new collective bargaining contract. Conciliators attempt to bring both sides together before time runs out.

As you can see from the minimal changes in the first case and significant changes in the second, the degree of simulation dictates how much role change is necessary in creating a new game.

Scenarios. The scenarios are the stories and settings built into a game. In MONOPOLY, there is a single, somewhat unrealistic but highly motivating scenario. Players are in a real estate world, where they buy properties and build on them in an attempt to become richer than the others. However, there are some restraining factors. Players go to jail, are assessed taxes, and so on. In instructional games dealing with urban planning, students create or reorganize cities.

Once again, as with roles, the amount of change required in scenarios depends on the degree of simulation in the game. Very straightforward drill-practice activities in math or foreign language require virtually no alteration of the scenario. RUMMY, as a frame, may be used to generate games where sets of three or four cards are combined based on the sums of numbers or classes of words, as shown in Figure 6. Because there are no elements of simulation in these games, there is no scenario. On the other hand, the NEEDS ANALYSIS GAME, which is a frame for selecting five high-priority consensus items, requires imaginative prepa-

Figure 6

Winning Rummy Combinations in RUMMATH

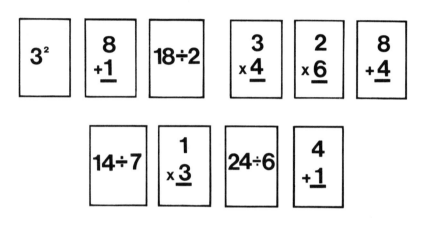

ration of scenarios. Briefly—since we shall return to this frame game in greater detail—here is what occurs:

Frame game: NEEDS ANALYSIS GAME
Role: A large group is broken into teams which deliberate on the high priority needs surrounding an issue. Through small-group discussion, lists of needs are generated. A consensus-forcing scoring system generates eventual agreement among all teams as to the five priority needs.

Adapted game 1: POLICY COUNCIL
Role: Players are important members of a policy council determining matters of starvation and food, birth and death for

the world. Each team represents a member of the policy council trying to reach consensus on the world food crisis. The council must determine what actions to implement to stave off imminent disaster.

Adapted game 2: FUTURE SCHOOL
Role: Players group themselves into committees—school board members, teachers, parents, recent graduates, administrators, community representatives—all trying to determine what changes might be made in the local school to meet the needs of a changing world. They must come up with a plan that all can support.

The key element in the design of roles and scenarios is imaginative credibility. Players have to believe the scenarios and fit into them comfortably. In POLICY COUNCIL, the opening scenario is presented in a highly credible manner, based on excerpts from current world food statistics. Players sense the urgency of the crisis. The CONFRONTATION game about campus conflict and the mediating role of campus ministers contains a number of scenarios taken from actual campus conflicts. The scenarios are, in fact, case histories slightly modified to fit the constraints of the game.

Scoring systems. Roles and scenarios may vary greatly from one game adaptation of a frame game to another, but as with the rules, scoring systems generally change very little. In both BINGO and TOOL BOX, five in a straight line wins. RUMMY variations usually use a scoring system in which you count the cards "remaining" against the player holding them. In the NEEDS ANALYSIS GAME, the consensus-forcing scoring system rewards teams which independently choose the same item. Generally speaking, then, scoring systems remain one of the least changed parts of a frame game. The method of determining winners and losers may require adjustment from the original game to its adaptations but is seldom radically altered.

Media. The way in which a game is packaged—printed or plasticized cards; pads or reusable writing surfaces; slick or cheap; print or slide-tape; plywood board or a cathode ray tube—depends on the nature of the objectives, the preferences of learners, the production resources, and the expertise of potential game runners. Media can be readily altered to accommodate the given content, learner group, and resources available. We have all played CONCENTRATION with ordinary playing cards. There are several television versions of the game with huge panels and computer controlled revolving cubes. There are children's electric board versions where two wires activate a flashing light. There are party-game versions in a cardboard box. Size, materials, and media differ, but the essential framework of chance pairing and spatial memory remains in all these different versions.

Designing Your Own Games from Frame Games

This section takes us into the actual design of instructional games from frame games. To do this, we use the time-honored method of teaching by example. The first part of this section examines five classic games and strips them down to their essential frames. The frames are then used to generate two divergent adaptations. The second part presents two frame games which have no content themselves, having been deliberately designed to permit easy loading, and demonstrates how new instructional games can be generated for widely differing settings. The final part presents a simulation frame game and then follows the same basic procedure. By the end of this section, you should be able to unload games to reveal their frames and then reload them with your own content.

Classic Games

This first part presents five well-known games. Each is described and then "unloaded" to reveal its basic frame. The frame is then utilized to generate two divergent "framed" instructional games.

CONCENTRATION

CONCENTRATION is a popular card game with many variations. Basically, the ordinary 52 playing card deck plus the two jokers is shuffled and then laid out, face down, in rows. Players take turns turning over cards two at a time, as illustrated in Figure 7. If they match—i.e., have the same value—the player turning the cards over keeps them and gets another turn. Players concentrate on the locations of different cards, since all unmatched cards are turned face down again. The winner is the player who collects the most cards.

Figure 7

CONCENTRATION

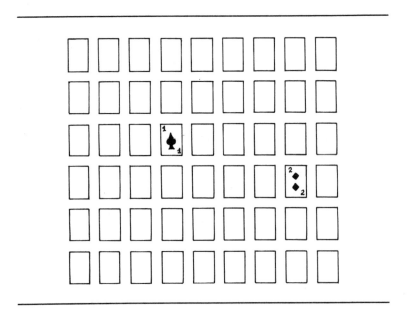

Removing the content from the game, we see that the concentration frame operates as follows:

1. Stimulus elements are randomly laid out with the faces hidden.
2. Players reveal two elements at a time.
3. Elements which form a pair are retained by the player. Elements which do not form a pair are turned face down.
4. Players take turns, unless a pair is revealed. A player uncovering a pair receives an extra turn.
5. Pairs are removed until no more elements remain.
6. Player with the highest number of pairs wins.

The CONCENTRATION frame is graphically depicted in Figure 8.

Adaptation 1. WEATHER WATCH
Players: Amateur sailors taking a course on weather.
Objective: Discriminate among various cloud forms.
Materials:

Forty cards with uniform backs containing photographs of various cloud forms. There are four different photographs of each of the following ten cloud forms: cirrus, cirro-cumulus, cirro-stratus, alto-cumulus, alto-stratus, nimbo-stratus, strato-cumulus, stratus, cumulus, cumulo-nimbus.
Number of players: Two to five.
Approximate time requirement: Fifteen to 20 minutes.
Play of the game:

1. The game leader shuffles all the cards and then places them face down in rows.

2. The first player selects two cards and turns them face up so that all players can see the cloud photographs on them.

3. If the two cards match, the player names the cloud form. The game leader verifies whether or not there is a match and whether the name is correct.

4. If correct, the player retains the pair and gets another turn. If incorrect (either through mismatching or misnaming), the game leader says "no" and play passes to the next player. If there is no match, play also passes on.

5. The game continues until all pairs are removed. The player with the most cards wins.

Figure 8

Basic Structure of CONCENTRATION

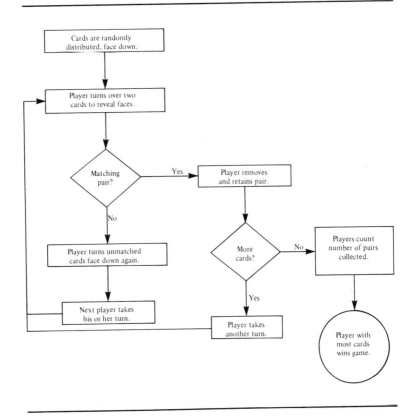

Adaptation 2. NUMBER VALUES
Players: Pre-school/primary school children.
Objective: Associate standard arabic numeral with its value.
Materials:
A standard set of dominoes (28).
Thirteen flashcards each containing a number from 0 to 12.
Number of players: Two to ten.
Approximate time requirement: Fifteen to 20 minutes.
Play of the game:
1. One child lays out all 28 dominoes in random fashion face down. Another child shuffles the 13 cards and also lays them out with the numbers hidden.
2. Players turn over one domino and one card at a time. If the number of dots on the face of the domino equals the number on the card, the player keeps the domino, but turns the card back over. If there is no match, both the card and the domino are turned back over. Players get an extra chance each time they make a match.
3. The game continues until all dominoes are removed from the table. The player with the highest number of dominoes wins the game.

KIM'S GAME

This is an old party game with a multitude of variations. Played with an ordinary deck of cards, essentially all of the cards are laid out face up in helter-skelter fashion. All but one player shut their eyes. The open-eyed player secretly removes a card from the table and then rearranges the cards. The other players open their eyes and attempt to identify the missing card. If no one guesses correctly, the card-removing player wins a point and gets another turn. If a player names the missing card correctly, he or she scores a point and gets to select the next card. The first player to score a given number of points wins the game.

Once again the structure of KIM'S GAME is graphically depicted in the flowchart in Figure 9. After unloading the playing cards' content, we are left with this basic frame:

Figure 9

Basic Structure of KIM'S GAME

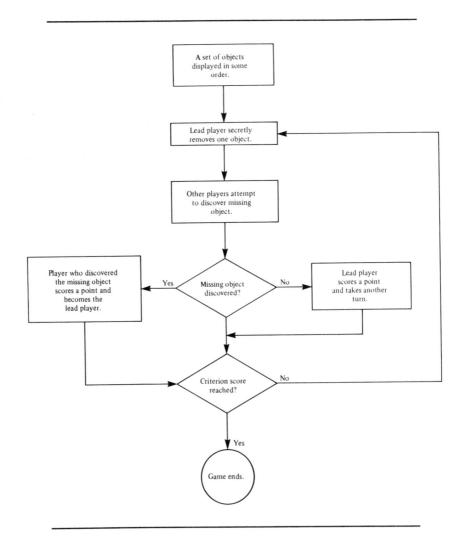

1. A large display of stimulus materials is arranged in random fashion.

2. One object is secretly removed and the display is then rearranged.

3. Players attempt to discover which object has been removed.

4. Play passes to the keenest observer.

Adaptation 1. CIRCUITRY

Players: Trainees in electronics assembly.

Objective: Note discrepancies between a wiring diagram and circuit board.

Materials:

Various circuit diagrams and correctly wired up boards with removable components.

Number of players: Four to six.

Approximate time requirement: Twenty to 30 minutes.

Play of the game:

1. One player selects a circuit diagram and the corresponding board that is wired correctly.

2. While other players study the diagram, the first player secretly removes a component and slightly rearranges the wiring within 60 seconds.

3. The other players attempt to locate what has been removed and rearranged. Each player gets only one chance within a time limit of three minutes.

4. If no one discovers the change, the first player scores a point and takes another turn with the same circuit board.

5. If one of the players spots what was removed and corrects it, he or she scores the point and replaces the first player, using a new circuit board.

6. First player to score seven points wins a game.

Adaptation 2. SET THE TABLE

Players: Upper elementary school children.

Objective: Set a table correctly.

Materials:

A table completely set with all plates, utensils, and napkins.

A second table with extra dishes, napkins, and silverware.

Number of players: Four to six.
Approximate time requirement: Ten minutes.
Play of the game:
  1. Children help the teacher set the table. Once the table is completely set, children walk around it, studying the arrangement.
  2. Children close their eyes and the teacher removes one article from the set table and places it among the extra items on the second table.
  3. Children open their eyes. The first child to identify the missing item names it. If he or she is right, he or she places it in the proper location, and scores a point.
  4. The winner of each round gets to remove the article for the next round.
  5. The first player to score ten points wins the game.

RUMMY

RUMMY is a popular card game that has evolved in different ways in different lands. Nevertheless, the basic RUMMY game begins with a shuffled deck from which a dealer distributes an equal number of cards to all players. The remaining cards form the bank. The top card of the bank is turned face up and placed next to the bank to start the discard pile. Players try to build up sets of cards—three or four of a kind or a sequence of the same length. Each player takes a turn to pick up an unknown card from the top of the bank or a known card from the discard pile and discards a card from his or her hand. The objective is to end up with sets of cards before other players do.

Here is the RUMMY frame:

1. Elements are randomly distributed to players. The remaining elements form a bank. A discard pile is started.

2. Players take turns drawing single elements from the bank or the discard pile and attempt to form sets and/or sequences of three or more. With each draw, there is a discard.

3. Play goes on until one player has combined all of his or her elements into appropriate sets.

4. Scoring is done by crediting the winning player with points from the losers.

5. The ultimate winner is the one who first reaches a predetermined score after a number of games.

Figure 10 shows the RUMMY frame in graphic form.

Adaptation 1. LES VERBES FRANCAIS

Players: Non-French-speaking adults in an intensive French course.

Objective: Recognize various verb families and their present affirmative endings.

Materials:

Cards with uniform backs and with infinitives or first, second, or third person singular or plural forms of selected verbs. There is a total of 84 cards consisting three each of verbs ending in -er, -ir, -oir, and -re in the infinitive and their singular and plural forms in the three persons.

Number of players: Two to six. Best game is for three or four.

Approximate time requirement: Fifteen to 20 minutes.

Play of the game:

1. Dealer shuffles the cards and deals ten to each player. Remaining cards are placed in a pile, face down, in the center of the table. One card from the pile is turned face up and placed to the side.

2. Players secretly arrange their hands into groups which fall into any of these categories:

Sets of three:

Three different infinitives.

First, second, third person singular or plural of same verb.

Three verbs of the same person and number.

Sets of four:

Four infinitives.

Infinitive and first, second, and third person singular of the same verb.

Four verbs of the same person and number.

Sets of six:

First, second, and third person singular and plural of the same verb.

Sets of seven:

Infinitive in addition to the six listed above.

3. Players take turns picking up the top card from either the

Figure 10

Basic Structure of RUMMY

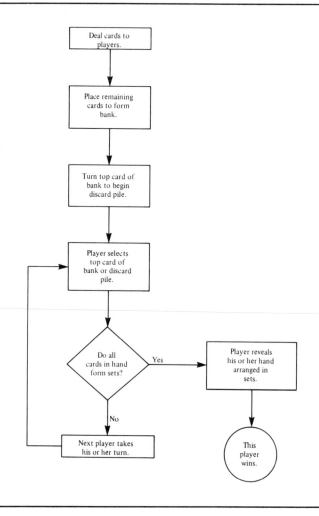

bank or the discard pile. They discard one card from their hands. During each turn, players rework their hands to make up more suitable sets.

4. As illustrated in Figure 11, a player can finish with two sets of three and one set of four; one set of six and one set of four; or one set of seven and one set of three. The first player to combine all cards in his or her hand into one of these combinations wins the game. He or she discards the last card face down and shouts "Finis!"

5. Players lay down their hands and count five points for each card which is not part of a permissible set. All these points are given to the winner.

Figure 11

Winning Combinations for LES VERBES FRANCAIS

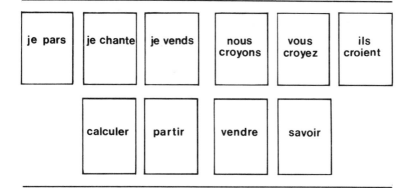

Adaptation 2. THE HOME
Players: First and second graders.
Objective: Match household objects with their names and the most likely part of the house in which they are found.
Materials:
Cards with pictures of household articles.
Cards with names of these articles.
Cards with names of different rooms.
For each picture card, there is a corresponding word card and

a room card. For example, one card contains the picture of a bed, another card the word "bed," and the third card the word "bedroom." About five sets of such cards are required. The deck contains two copies of each card, giving us a total of 30 cards.

Number of players: Two to four.

Approximate time requirement: Fifteen to 30 minutes.

Play of the game:

1. The object of the game is to get a set of three cards. For example, a set may contain the following cards:

Picture of an oven.

The word "oven."

The word "kitchen."

2. One player shuffles all the cards and gives each player five cards. The remaining cards are placed face down in the middle of the table. The top card of this pile is placed face up beside it.

3. The players take turns to do the following:

a. Take either the top card from the face-down pile or the face-up card beside it.

b. Place this card with other cards in the hand.

c. Remove any card which is not useful for making a set and place it face-up on top of the other face-up cards.

4. Play continues until a player collects a three-card set to win the game.

TIC-TAC-TOE

Moving away from frame games with cards, we come to one of the oldest, most popular, and durable of all games: TIC-TAC-TOE. As shown in Figure 12, this simple game pits two players against each other as they attempt to place three X's or O's in a line vertically, horizontally, or diagonally on a 3 x 3 matrix.

Figure 13 graphically reveals the TIC-TAC-TOE frame. The following narrative description of its structure is perhaps less complex sounding:

1. A 3 x 3 grid is drawn.

2. Each player is assigned a different symbol.

3. Players take turns placing individual symbols on the grid.

Figure 12

TIC-TAC-TOE Win

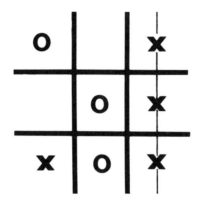

4. Players maneuver to line up their own symbols horizontally, vertically, or diagonally while preventing the opponent from doing the same.

5. The first player to successfully line up three symbols wins.

In the basic game of TIC-TAC-TOE, players choose any vacant cell. By requiring them to work for their choice of the cell, we can create motivating, instructional games. The following two adaptations illustrate this.

Adaptation 1. THIS WILL KILL YOU
Players: Adults enrolled in a consumer health education course.
Objective: Name the highest-probability health hazards for specific age, race, and sex groups.
Materials:
A game board on an overhead transparency which looks like the one shown in Figure 14.

Figure 13

Basic Structure of TIC-TAC-TOE

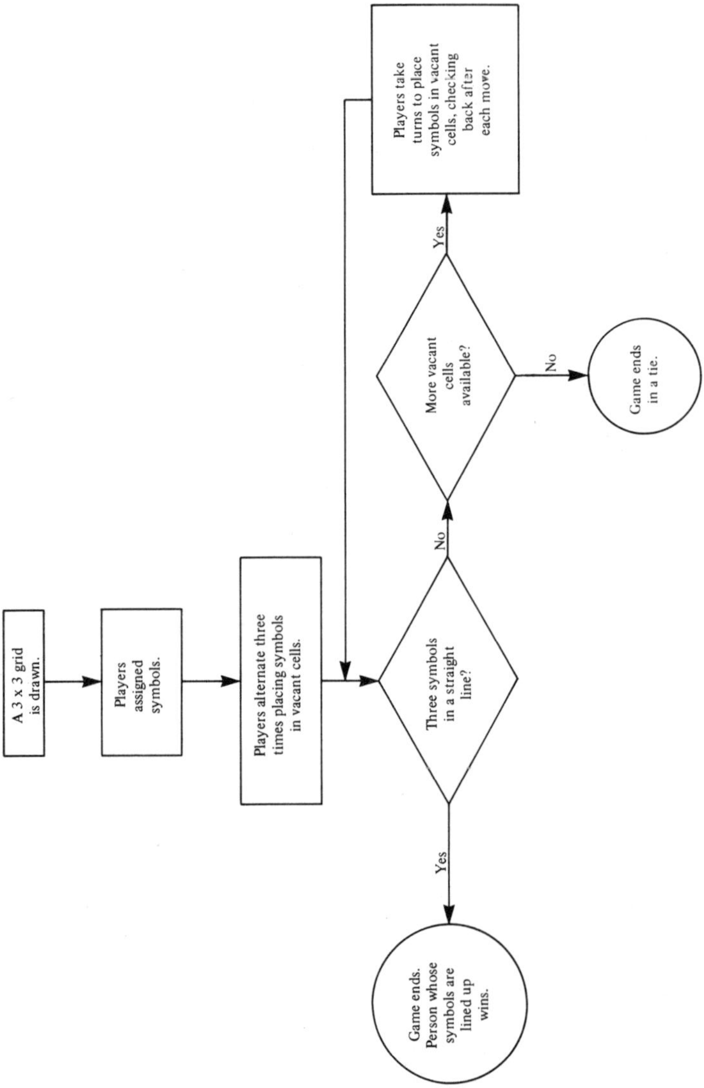

Figure 14

"THIS WILL KILL YOU"

	BLACK ♀	BLACK ♂	WHITE ♀	WHITE ♂	
7					7
17					17
37					37
57					57
	BLACK ♀	BLACK ♂	WHITE ♀	WHITE ♂	

A set of cutout X's and O's.

A summary of the Geller tables which lists the top ten health hazards for each sub-group shown in the matrix.

Media equipment: An overhead projector and a screen.

Number of players: Two teams of up to seven players each. Others may serve as a TV audience and vicariously participate in the game.

Approximate time requirement: Thirty to 40 minutes.

Play of the game:

1. The game leader, acting as a TV host, selects two teams of players. Rest of the class applauds and generally acts as a TV audience.

2. The game leader assigns X to one team and O to the other team.

3. The X team takes the first turn. It selects a cell by defining age, race, and sex. Team members collaboratively select what they consider to be the most probable killer for that particular group.

4. The opposing team may challenge the selection by offering any alternative health hazard which they consider to be a higher-probability cause of death.

5. If there is no challenge, the killer named by the first team

must be the highest cause of death reported in the Geller tables for the team to win the cell. If there is a challenge, the team with the higher-probability killer wins the right to place its symbol in that cell.

6. Play swings back and forth between teams as each names a cell, selects what it considers to be the highest-probability killer for that age-race-sex group, and wins or loses the right to place its symbols on the cell.

7. As illustrated in Figure 15, play continues until one team places three X's or O's in a line, vertically, horizontally, or diagonally to win the game.

Figure 15

The "X" Team Wins

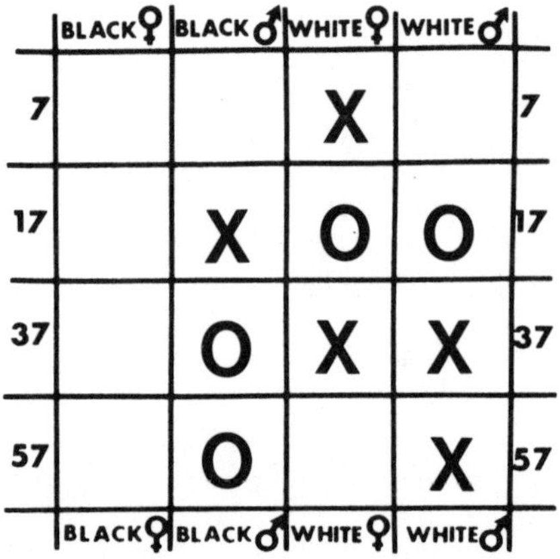

Adaptation 2. SAFETY RULES
Players: School children participating in a safety campaign sponsored by the local police.
Objective: Observe safety rules for home, school, and street.
Materials:
   A game board in the form of a large 3 x 3 grid. Each row

stands for a different place where safety rules should be practiced: home, school, and street. Each column represents different difficulty levels of questions: easy, medium, and hard. (See Figure 16.)

Figure 16

"SAFETY RULES"

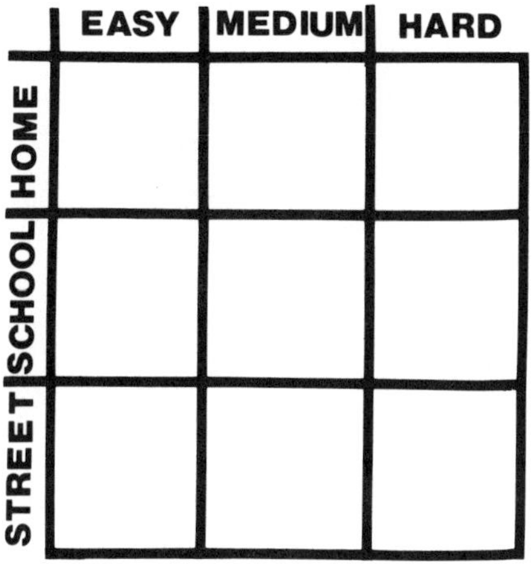

At least five cards with individual questions about the three safety situations at each of the three levels of difficulty. The correct answer to each question is found on the back of the card.

Two sets of counters of different colors.

Number of players: Two. If there are more players, the game is played in teams.

Approximate time requirement: Five to ten minutes.

Play of the game:

1. The first player selects one of the squares on the grid. The other player pulls out a suitable question card. For example, the first player wants the middle square. The other player finds a card with a medium-level question about safety at school.

2. The first player reads the question and gives the answer. The other player checks it with the answer on the back of the card.

3. If the answer is correct, the player places one of his or her counters on the appropriate square. If incorrect, nobody occupies the square.

4. The second player now chooses a square. The first player finds him or her a suitable question card. The game is played as before.

5. The object of the game is to place three counters of the same color in a straight line horizontally, vertically, or diagonally. The player to do so wins the game.

SNAKES AND LADDERS

This is an old English moralistic game which has enjoyed immense popularity among families in many English-speaking countries outside the USA. Generally, two to five players compete in a race to the top using dice to advance along a board which looks like the one shown in Figure 17. A player

Figure 17

"SNAKES AND LADDERS" Gameboard

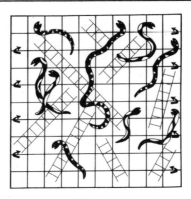

landing on a square which contains the foot of a ladder may climb it, thus gaining a bonus advance. If a player lands on a square containing a snake's head, he or she is swallowed and drops to the tail. In the Victorian versions, various squares contain Biblical sayings or pious homilies. The winner is the first one to reach the last (usually the 100th) square. (If a player arrives at the end and has too high a throw on the dice, he or she advances to 100, then continues the count as he or she retreats. Even at the top row, a player can be swallowed by the "serpent of evil."

The SNAKES AND LADDERS frame is shown in Figure 18 and described below.

1. Players use a random number generator (usually a pair of dice) to advance along a sequential path toward a goal.

2. Players take turns to move on the board. Landing on specific squares may either provide a shortcut or a backslide.

3. The first player to reach the final square exactly wins the game.

Adaptation 1. DRIVING TEST

Players: Driver trainees who have completed basic driving theory.
Objective: Select the correct actions in driving a car through a simulated driving test.
Materials:

A game board consisting of ten rows of ten squares simulating a winding roadway with a number of shortcuts, detours, obstacles, and traffic signals.

Two series of cards, one labeled *car trouble*, the other, *road problems*.

Small plastic cars.

A spinner in the shape of a speedometer.

Number of players: Two to six.
Approximate time requirement: Twenty to 40 minutes.
Play of the game:

1. Each player, in turn, spins the spinner and advances one square for each ten miles per hour.

2. If a player lands on a shortcut square, he or she may

Figure 18

Basic Structure of SNAKES AND LADDERS

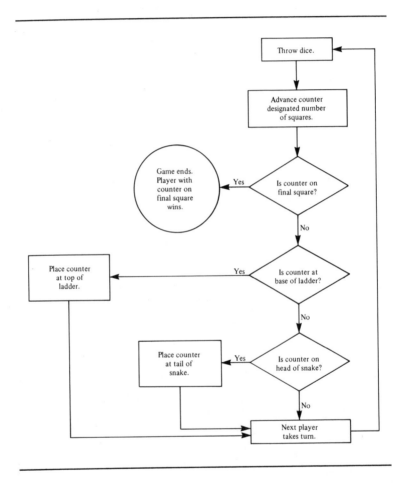

advance to the end of the shortcut. If a player stops on a detour square, he or she must turn and go to the end of the detour.

3. When a player lands on a *car trouble* square, another player draws a *car trouble* card and reads the question. If the player who has car trouble answers correctly, he or she receives bonus turns. Incorrect answers result in breakdowns or engine stalls which result in losing turns.

4. A player with three errors fails the test. He or she returns to the first square and begins again.

5. Play continues until one player parks his or her car successfully on the last square and wins a driver's license.

Adaptation 2. TELLING TIME
Players: Elementary school children.
Objective: Tell time correctly to the nearest five minutes from a standard clock.
Materials:

The game board is a spiral arrangement with clock faces as shown in Figure 19. In the elementary version of this game, the clock faces show one through 12 o'clock in a random order.

Figure 19

"TELLING TIME"

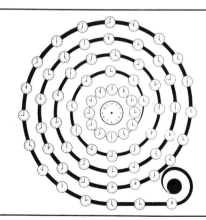

Twelve language master cards each with an audio recording of one of the 12 times shown on the clock faces. (There are no visual cues on the cards.)

Each player uses a poker chip of a different color as his or her piece.

Number of players: Two to five.

Approximate time requirement: Twenty to 30 minutes.

Play of the game:

1. One child (winner of the previous game) is designated as the game leader. This child shuffles the language master cards at the beginning of each round.

2. Each player picks a card from the leader's hand. They take turns to play their card on the language master machine and move their poker chip ahead to the first clockface with the specified time.

3. After all players have played their cards and moved their pieces, the next round begins. Players return their cards to the leader who repeats the same procedure.

4. The game ends when a player lands on one of the clock faces in the middle.

New Frame Games

While the time-tested, classic games of the types described above provide highly motivating and useful frames, game designers are continually designing new frame games into which different instructional content can be easily loaded. The list below contains some of the more flexible frame games of recent origin:

Amberstone, A., and Amberstone, W. THE POWER GAME

Armstrong, R.H.R., and Hobson, N. NEXUS

Coppard, L.C. POLICYPLAN

Duke, R.D., Becker, H., and Greenblat, C.S. CONFER-ENCE GAMES

Duke, R.D., and Greenblat, C.S. AT-ISSUE

Duke, R.D., and Greenblat, C.S. CONCEPTUAL MAP-PING GAME

Duke, R.S., and Greenblat, C.S. IMPASSE

Duke, R.D., and Stenber, N. GENERAL SYSTEMS GAME

Fennessey, G.M., and Schild, E.O. INFORMATION

Horn, A. A GAME FACILITATOR

Horn, A., and Goodman, F.L. RUMMAGING

Horn, A., and Steinwachs, B. PIECE OF MIND

Instructional Simulations, Inc. SYSTEM I

Klietsch, R.G. ORACLE-QUEST-ORDER

Tombaugh, R.F., and Davis, J. PX-190

Twelker, P.A. CONDUCTING PLANNING EXERCISES

Descriptions of any of these frame games and additional information about their availability may be obtained from Robert E. Horn's *The Guide to Simulations/Games for Education and Training* (see "Resources"). In addition, the book on TEAMS-GAMES-TOURNAMENT in this series also deals with an instructional design format which may be considered as a higher-order frame game.

In this section, we describe two new frame games of our own creation. Because the original versions have almost no content, they are very briefly described. Following the description of each frame game are two adaptations dealing with two different instructional content and player groups. These adaptations are described in some detail, along with sample segments from actual play of the game, in order to provide comprehensive models for your own efforts in adapting them to suit local instructional needs.

NEEDS ANALYSIS GAME

This frame game is appropriate for situations where a prioritized list of some kind is required. This game receives inputs from members of a group, and through a scoring system which rewards consensus, produces a prioritized list of needs, criteria, products, people, principles, action steps, etc.

The basic structure of the game is shown in Figure 20 and described as follows:

1. The group is divided into teams of four to six players.

2. Each team prepares a list of policies, positions, needs (or whatever), that is appropriate to the topic.

3. Once the teams have prepared their lists, the game leader elicits one item from each team and writes it on a chalkboard or flip-chart. This process is continued until a dozen items get listed in this common list.

4. Each team secretly selects the most acceptable item.

5. Team selections are exposed. Teams score a point for every team selecting the same item.

6. The item which receives the most votes is ranked first and crossed off the list.

7. The game continues until a pre-specified number of items is selected.

Adaptation 1. THE POLICY COUNCIL GAME

What would it feel like to be an important member of a policy council determining matters of starvation and food, birth and death, and a host of other critical factors? Every day, different councils debate food, population, energy, and agricultural policies all over the world, from local meetings of village elders somewhere in rural Chad to large assemblies of sophisticated diplomats in the United Nations. These key decision-makers have to come up with policies in the best interests of the most people.

In the following simulation game, each team represents a member of a policy council trying to reach consensus on vital issues related to the world food problem. During the play of the game, you experience some of the frustrations in trying to reconcile what you feel is the best policy with what others are willing to accept. Your team scores high if it comes up with widely accepted solutions and also if it accepts stronger solutions from other teams.

Players: Adults interested in the world food problem.

Objective: Identify five acceptable policies which can help alleviate the world food problem.

Number of players: Three to 30. If there are five or fewer, each

Figure 20

Basic Structure of NEEDS ANALYSIS GAME

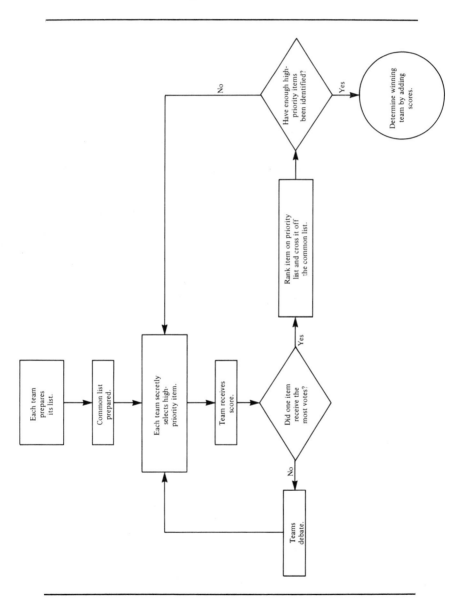

plays individually. With more than five, players are divided into three to six teams of approximately equal numbers.
Approximate time requirement: One to two hours.
Materials:
    Paper and pencil for each team.
    Chalkboard or a large flip-chart for writing down the common list of policies.
Play of the game:
    The following are brief descriptions of the steps in the game. Each step is illustrated by the outcomes from an actual game played by a group of adults. The steps in the game are printed in regular type while the sample game segments are printed in italics.
    1. *Preliminaries.* The game leader divides the players into a suitable number of teams. He or she briefly explains that the teams are about to participate in a policy council meeting, specifies the issue on which policies are to be set, and provides background information about the context in which the meeting takes place.
    There are 23 players and Fred, our game leader, divides them into five teams. Three teams end up with five players and the other two with four, but this does not matter. Fred explains that they are about to simulate the deliberations of the presidential advisory commission of a small developing nation in Southeast Asia. This nation has a rapidly growing population rate which is holding up their drive toward self-sufficiency in food production. The council is given the task of coming up with policies for reducing the birth rate in the country.
    2. *Generating individual lists.* Each team prepares a list of five suggested policies in the specified areas. Members of each team collaborate with each other in this task, but no team is permitted to consult with another team.
    Fred explains what is to be done during the first phase of the game. He suggests that the teams work fast because there is a ten-minute time limit for coming up with a list of policies. Here are the lists generated by different teams:

Alan's team:
    1. Encourage national research in inexpensive and reliable contraceptive devices.
    2. Distribute birth control pills at a subsidized rate to working women in urban areas.
    3. Strongly encourage women to undergo sterilization when they are in the hospitals to deliver babies.

4. Introduce lessons on the dangers of rapid population growth in the elementary and high school curricula.

5. Produce documentary films on the plight of large families.

Barbara's team:

1. Concentrate on educating rural women on the advantages of having a small family.

2. Implement compulsory vasectomy of men with more than three children.

3. Improve infant health care so that babies have greater chances of living.

4. Increase job opportunities for women.

5. Deny promotion of civil servants with more than three children.

Charlie's team:

1. Make surgical sterilization of men and women freely available.

2. Deny government-subsidized housing to large families.

3. Develop a system of old age pension so that senior citizens are not dependent upon their children.

4. Train a large army of family planning workers to spread the message in rural areas.

5. Concentrate on the use of the IUD loop on a large scale.

Diana's team:

1. Relax abortion laws.

2. Mobilize religious opinion in favor of birth control.

3. Undertake a concentrated media blitz on birth control.

4. Offer financial incentives to parents with few children (e.g., negative income tax exemptions).

5. Supply contraceptive devices free-of-charge to poor people in villages.

Esther's team:

1. Encourage men to undergo vasectomies.

> *2. Widely disseminate information on contraceptive techniques.*
>
> *3. Offer cash incentives to moviemakers who produce feature films about family planning.*
>
> *4. Make contraceptive devices freely and widely available to anyone who needs it.*
>
> *5. Discourage large families by increasing the financial burden on the parents.*

3. *Creating a common list.* The game leader asks each team to read aloud one suggested policy from its list which he or she writes on the chalkboard. Teams try to contribute policies which are different from those already on the list. This procedure is continued until the common list on the chalkboard contains ten policy suggestions.

Alan's team starts off the common list with the first policy from their list. Fred summarizes it on the chalkboard. Other teams take turns to contribute their policies to the common list, which ends up with the following ten items:

1. *Encourage research on contraception.*
2. *Increase job opportunities for women.*
3. *Wide dissemination of contraceptive information.*
4. *Media propaganda blitz.*
5. *Free surgical sterilization.*
6. *Cheap birth control pills.*
7. *Compulsory vasectomy.*
8. *Old age pension.*
9. *Free contraceptives.*
10. *Financial burdens on parents of large families.*

4. *Selecting the most acceptable policy.* Each team now studies the common list and selects the one policy which it believes to be the most acceptable one to different people. The game leader secretly collects the choices of each team and announces them after all teams have decided.

During this phase, Alan's and Esther's teams chose Item 6 ("Cheap birth control pills"). Charlie's and Barbara's chose Item 3 ("Wider dissemination"), and Diana's team chose Item 5 ("Free surgical sterilization").

5. *Scoring the round.* The game leader computes a score for each team which equals the number of teams selecting the same policy. (This score rewards consensus.)

Scores for the teams at the end of the first round are two each for Alan's, Esther's, Barbara's, and Charlie's teams and one for Diana's team.

6. *Ranking the policy.* The policy which receives the most choices is crossed off the common list and given the first rank for acceptability. If more than one policy receives the same high number of choices, no policy is ranked. The players are given a brief debate period during which they elaborate upon the relative merits of their choices and try to persuade each other. Then the teams return to another round of secret selection during which they can stay with their original choice or shift to a new policy.

No policy is crossed off at the end of the first round because of the tie between Items 3 and 6 with two votes each. There is a two-minute debate period during which various persuasive points are made: "People don't know anything about contraception. You've got to teach them it is possible." "Surgery is more reliable than the pill and it is guaranteed to bring down the birth rate." During the ensuing round, Alan's team shifts to Item 2. Esther's team shifts from Item 6 to Item 3 and joins Charlie's and Barbara's. Diana's team stays with the original choice of free sterilization. This gives the following scores to the team for the second round: Barbara, Charlie, and Esther, three each; and Alan and Diana, one each.

7. *Recycling.* After crossing off the first ranked policy from the common list, the game procedure is repeated for identifying the next four most acceptable policies, one at a time. During each round, the teams make confidential choices and the game leader reveals them and announces scores. The policy which receives the most votes during each round is crossed off the common list.

The game proceeds according to the rules for five more rounds to determine the next four acceptable policies. (One of the rounds ends in a two-way tie.) At the end of this phase, the five selected policies are:
- *Wider dissemination of contraceptive information.*
- *Free surgical sterilization.*
- *Financial burdens on parents of large families.*
- *Increase job opportunities for women.*
- *Research on contraception.*

8. *Determining the winners.* The game comes to an end when the top five policies have been identified. Each team adds up its score points accumulated during the earlier rounds of voting; the team with the highest score wins the game.

In addition to winning the game on this consensus score, teams may compare their performance on another criterion. Each team checks its original list of five policy suggestions against the top five policies identified from the common list. The team which has more of its original suggestions (or reasonable facsimiles thereof) among the top five are declared to be the winners.

Total scores for the different teams are 16 each for Alan's and Diana's, 18 for Esther's, 20 for Charlie's, and 22 for Barbara's team. Hence, Barbara's team is declared the winner in the consensus category. Esther's original list is found to contain three policies which made the top five. Her team wins an award for this.

Variations

1. The length of this game can be shortened by reducing the number of policies. For example, you may require each team to list three policies and make a common list with six, from which the top three are to be selected.

2. Another way to speed up the game is do away with the first phase, during which each team generates its own list. You can begin with a ready-made list of ten policies and have the teams identify the top five using the procedure in the latter phase of the game.

Suggested Alternative Topics:

- Nutritional policy of a developing nation.
- Fuel policy in a developed nation.
- International policy about weather modification.
- International policy about harvesting the seas.
- Agricultural credit policy of a federal bank in a developing region.

Adaptation 2. AFFECT ANALYSIS

Players: Elementary school teachers.

Objective: Identify an attitudinal goal and convert it into a behavioral objective by specifying suitable indicators.

Materials:

Chalkboard and chalk.

Paper and pencils.

Approximate time requirement: Sixty to 90 minutes.

Play of the game:

1. Teams cooperatively select a goal statement. *"Children shall take pride in their work."*

2. Each team lists *five* behavioral indicators of this attitudinal goal.

Team A:
1. *Desks are tidy and neat.*
2. *Children do more work than is assigned to them.*
3. *Classroom has on display work done by different children.*
4. *Children listen attentively while peers describe their work.*
5. *Many trophies and awards decorate classroom.*

Team B:
1. *Children choose own activities.*
2. *Children work independently.*
3. *Children readily talk about their work to teacher.*
4. *Children share ideas and skills with each other.*
5. *Children save their projects to show parents.*

Team C:
1. *Children show their work to teacher voluntarily.*
2. *Children talk about details of their work with others.*
3. *Children keep their work clean and protect it carefully.*
4. *Children get upset if their product is damaged or destroyed.*
5. *Children show their work to others.*

3. A consolidated list of different indicators is prepared from individual team lists and displayed on the blackboard.

1. *Children show their work to teacher and talk about it.*
2. *Children show their work to their peers and talk about it.*
3. *Children show their work to their parents and talk about it.*
4. *Children listen to other people's descriptions of their work.*
5. *Children protect their work carefully and keep it clean.*
6. *Children get upset if their work is damaged or destroyed.*
7. *Children choose their own activities.*

> *8. Children work beyond teacher's demands.*
> *9. Children show indicators of achievement (trophies, grades, gold stars, etc.) to others.*

4. Teams secretly select the most widely acceptable indicator from this list and write down its identification number. Teams compare their selections and give themselves a score equal to the number of teams selecting the same indicators.

> *Team A and Team C chose the fifth indicator. Team B chose the second one. Scores: Team A = 2, Team B = 1, Team C = 2.*

5. The indicator selected by the most teams is eliminated; the teams now select the second most widely acceptable indicator. This process of selection and scoring is repeated until the top five are identified. In case of ties, no indicator is eliminated and tie-breaking rounds are played until one item emerges with more selections than the other.

> *These are the final ranks as determined by the three teams:*

Rank	Indicator
I	5
II	8
III	1
IV	6
V	9

6. The team with the top selection score wins the award for recognizing popular indicators. The team which has the most number of the top five indicators in its original list wins the award for being able to generate the most acceptable indicators.

> *Team scores when the top five were located:*

Team A	16
Team B	17
Team C	15

Team B wins this part of the game.

Comparing the top five indicators with the original listings of each team, we see Team A with two of them, Team B with one of them, and Team C with two of them. So Teams A and C tie for being the most generative.

GROUP GROPE

This simple frame game can generate a great deal of activity, enthusiasm, and loud discussions. It is designed for large groups and has been used with success in a wide variety of settings—a workshop for the hard-core unemployed, an evening gathering of the elderly, a fourth-grade class in social studies, a seminar of dentists on occupational stress. The basic, stripped down structure of GROUP GROPE is shown in Figure 21 and described as follows:

1. Opinion cards around a given topic are prepared.

2. Players receive five opinion cards.

3. Players discard opinion cards they do not like and replace them with better ones from a bank.

4. Players exchange cards to improve their hands.

5. Players form coalitions with people holding similar opinions.

6. Groups prepare summary statements and name themselves.

7. Game leader awards prizes.

This frame not only helps players examine a range of opinions on a given topic, but also to find kindred souls and plan a mutual course of action.

Adaptation 1. THE COCKTAIL PARTY

Have you ever noticed how people with similar opinions tend to cluster together during a cocktail party? The following game speeds up the process of identifying kindred souls with similar opinions on world food problems. This game is ideal for an actual cocktail party, but you can create sufficient enthusiasm even in the absence of any refreshments.

Players: An action group concerned about world food problems.

Objective: Increase the awareness of the range of opinions regarding world food problems.

Number of players: Ten to 60. This is one of those games where the more players you have, the merrier it becomes.

Approximate time requirement: Thirty minutes to an hour.

Figure 21

Basic Structure of GROUP GROPE

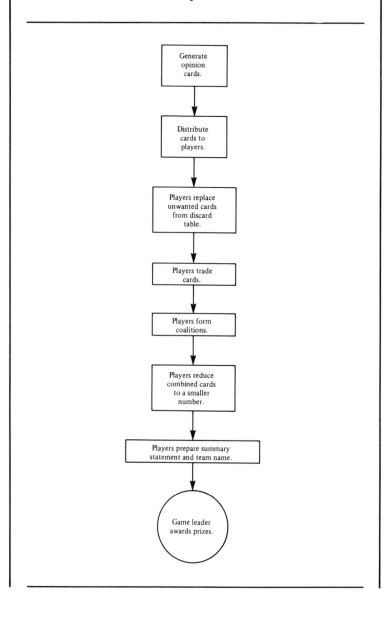

Materials:
A set of opinion cards, six per player.
Play of the game:
The following are brief descriptions of the steps in the game. Each step is illustrated by the outcomes from an actual game played by a group of students. The steps in the game are printed in regular type while the sample game segments are printed in italics.

1. *Preliminaries.* Long before the game is scheduled, the game leader prepares a set of opinion cards. These cards contain statements about some selected aspect of world food problems representing the entire gamut of opinions, from the positive to the neutral to the negative. At least five opinion cards should be prepared for each expected player. Ideally, each opinion must be different from the others, but if a large number of players is expected, duplicate cards may be used.

Peggy is organizing a consciousness raising session for the local women's group. She selects the broad topic of world food problems and sits down to write different opinions on 3 x 5 cards. Among the pungent statements she makes are the following:

"There is enough food for everyone, if only we knew how to share."

"Dog food in the USA contains more nutrition than what half of the world's children get!"

"Stop wheat exports to Russia."

"It is the middle man who makes a big profit."

"Skip a meal every week!"

"Prevent people pollution: Practice birth control!"

"Small is beautiful: Support the small farmer!"

"Support basic research in agriculture!"

"There is plenty of protein in the seas!"

2. *Receiving the initial hand.* Each player is given a random set of five opinion cards. The players read the cards and decide with which ones they agree. Five minutes are allotted for this purpose.

The game is scheduled for 7 p.m. and people begin drifting in just before that time. Peggy distributes a set of five cards to each person as she enters. After everyone is assembled, Peggy explains what they are to do with the cards. All of the 32 players study their cards. Cathy, one of the players, has these cards:

"Bring down meat prices through selective boycott!"

"Reduce your consumption of meat. Plant protein is easier to produce!"

"Send your contribution to CARE so that they can send food to starving children!"

"Birth rates in poor nations will go down when the status of women goes up."

"Stop foreign aid to undeserving nations."

She does not particularly care for any of them, and she detests the first and the last ones especially.

3. *Discarding and replacement.* The game leader leaves extra opinion cards on a table in the middle of the room. During the second phase of the game, players may discard any cards from their hand which they do not like and pick up replacements. Ten minutes are allotted for this task.

Cathy takes her hand to the table and rummages among the cards there. She replaces her meat-boycott card with another one which says, "Let's share our agricultural know-how with developing nations." She also picks up another card which says, "There is plenty of uncultivated land all around the world" and throws out the one which suggests stopping all foreign aid. She is shocked to see Martha eagerly picking up the card she has discarded.

4. *Group formation.* Players are asked to compare their cards with each other. During this phase, any player may exchange any of his or her cards with those of the others. In addition, players with similar opinion cards can form a coalition. Members of the coalition may throw out any card from their combined hands if they do not agree with them. There is no limit to the number of people who team together.

Cathy goes around the room checking with others and trading cards. She runs across Ellen, who has five excellent cards, and they decide to team up together. The two of them set out to find other kindred souls. Nancy wants to join them, and Cathy and Ellen agree to let her in on the condition that she drops the card which says, "Compulsory sterilization is the only way to curb a population explosion." In about 20 minutes, this group incorporates ten happy players.

5. *Group decisions.* The game leader announces the end of the coalition formation phase and requires each group to come up with a name and a brief statement summarizing its opinions. After ten minutes, each group is to share the name and the statement with the others.

At the end of 15 minutes, Peggy, the game leader, flicks the lights on and off to catch people's attention. She announces that they are to stop expanding their groups and to decide upon a name for their group and a summary statement. There are five groups in the room, ranging from a small one of three to Cathy's group, which is the largest one, with 11 members. Members of this group divide themselves into two sub-groups, one to pick an appropriate name and the other to write the summary statement. They eventually select "Cautious Optimists" as their name. Their statement reads, "We believe that there is an urgent problem related to the production and distribution of food all around the world, especially in specific areas of Asia, Africa, and Latin America. While this calls for careful study and collaborative problem-solving among all people of the world, we do not currently consider there is any need for panic." When it is their turn, Cathy announces the group's name and reads the carefully worded statement.

6. *The awards ceremony.* The leader brings the game to a close by recognizing the biggest and the smallest groups and presenting appropriate awards for different outcomes.

Peggy chooses her categories for the awards in such a way that all groups get an award of some sort. Even the group which came up with an atrocious name and an ambiguous statement gets special recognition for being the group with room for the greatest improvement!

Variations

1. Instead of preparing the opinion cards beforehand, the game leader may ask each player to write five opinions on blank cards at the beginning of the game. These cards are then shuffled and distributed to the players.

2. Instead of asking the groups to write their opinion statements, they may be asked to choose two cards from their common collection which best represents their stand.

Suggested Alternative Topics

The following are some suggested replacements for the topic of world food problems used in the sample game. You can come up with your own topic which best suits the needs of your players.

- Foreign aid to developing nations.
- Effects of the expanding population.
- The energy crisis and the food problem.
- Food prices and inflation.
- Land reform to increase food production.

Adaptation 2. OUR SCHOOL

This adaptation has a twist to it. The main purpose is to focus students' attention on their school so that they can suggest ways of improving it.

Players: Middle school students.

Objective: Share opinions on how to improve the school and generate action plans.

Number of players: Any number from 15 to 50.

Materials:

Index cards with a wide range of suggestions on how to improve the school.

Approximate time requirement: One hour.

Play of the game:

1. Student reporters spend a week interviewing students, school personnel, parents, and community leaders for their opinions on how to improve the school. Each opinion is written on an index card.

Mary, Mark, and Beth gather a wide range of suggestions which they transfer to cards, one at a time. Some of the opinions read as follows:

- *Clean up the grounds.*
- *Monitor corridors between classes.*
- *Fire all the teachers.*
- *Bring back compulsory study hall.*
- *Organize more community activities in the school.*
- *Organize an escort service for girls walking home late.*

2. Five cards are randomly distributed to each student player.

Robbie gets the following cards:

- *Start a safety patrol.*
- *Raise money for new football sweaters.*
- *Set up a volunteer tutoring service for students with difficulties.*
- *Change the principal.*
- *Work out activities to help integration.*

3. Players unload cards they do not want on a discard table and pick up others lying on the table.

Robbie gets rid of two cards and rummages around until he finally selects:

- *Invite a kid from another race, religion, or country, home.*
- *Organize more community activities in the school.*

He adds these to his other three.

4. Players wander around exchanging cards and forming coalitions with other players.

Robbie meets Carlos and Pete, who seem to have good cards. They trade with Robin and Elsa. As they wander around trading, they find that they have ten cards all relating to the improvement of race relations. Surprisingly, Ida-Jean (sometimes known as "The Snob") decides to join their coalition.

5. Player coalitions select names for the teams. Each team then prepares a statement of action that it would like to see implemented to improve the school.

Robbie, Carlos, Pete, and Ida-Jean put their heads together. After some heated debate, they decide on the team name of the "Martin Luther Kings." Their statement reads as follows:

"This school is only as good as the people getting along with each other. There are too many separate groups that are afraid of each other. We want to see different groups doing things together, inviting each other to their homes, organizing ethnic shows, trading recipes, clothes, getting smarter students to tutor slower ones, and working on projects that break down prejudice."

6. The entire group, under the guidance of the teacher, works out ways various groups can implement their ideas. Prizes are given to the group which implements the most actions, the most significant actions, and the most difficult action within a specific time period.

Robbie and friends decide to meet again after school and organize a tutoring program as a first step toward improved group relations.

Simulation Games

Although some of the classic and new frame games we described earlier had a few elements of simulation in them, none of them were an instructional simulation game which was deliberately designed to achieve objectives related to the process being simulated. For more details on the design, development, and use of instructional simulation games, you may want to read the authors' book on that topic in this series. Below, we describe a frame game of the simulation variety to show how the same design principles apply. As before, our frame game is followed by two adaptations. As you study these adaptations, notice how the scenarios and roles change considerably.

IDIOTS (Instructional Development in Ordinary Teaching Situations)

IDIOTS is a simulation game designed to sensitize instructional technologists to various interpersonal aspects of working with subject-matter experts during the systematic development of training materials.

Number of players: Two. The game is designed for parallel play by a large number of pairs. The game can thus handle up to about 25 pairs playing simultaneously.

Time requirement: Thirty to 45 minutes.

Materials:

A printed scenario.

Issues cards deck.

Poker chips.

Paper and pencil.

Play of the game:

1. *Preliminaries.* Players are divided into pairs. Each pair is given a deck of issues cards and each individual player is given a copy of the background scenario and an unspecified number of poker chips (usually five to 15). The game leader also announces the time limit for the game.

2. *Providing the context.* Each player reads his or her copy of the scenario which describes the context in which a series of interpersonal confrontations takes place. This scenario outlines the mission for both players and the role of each, as in the following example:

> You and the other player are involved in an instructional development project in a university setting. The purpose of this project is to produce an instructional package to teach certain specific skills to undergraduate students.
>
> The professor involved in the project is a subject-matter expert (SME). He or she knows very little about instructional design or media production. In addition to working on the project, he or she has a half-time teaching load.

The instructional developer (ID) involved in the project has considerable experience in designing different types of training packages and producing mediated materials. However, he or she has very little knowledge of the content area. In addition to work on the project, he or she has the regular duties of coordinating the learning resources center in the school.

The winner of a coin toss chooses one of the two roles. The other player assumes the other role.

3. *Identifying issues.* One player turns over the top card of the issues deck. This deck contains 30 cards, each describing an issue and five different positions arranged along a five-point scale, as in the following example:

ISSUE: Working arrangements.
POSITIONS:
1. The SME outlines the content and suggests different resource materials. The ID will do most of the actual development.
2. The SME provides initial guidance and periodic supervision as the ID develops the instructional material.
3. The SME and the ID share equal responsibilities and keep in close touch with each other.
4. The SME develops the instructional material with periodic suggestions and help from the ID.
5. The SME does most of the development. The ID serves in consultative and editorial capacities.

Other cards deal with such issues as the use of behavioral objectives, sharing of credits, selection of media, need for evaluation, and hiring of the staff. Both players read the statement and the five positions on the issue.

4. *Indicating initial position.* Each player now individually writes down a number indicating his or her initial position on the issue. After both players have done so, they compare

their positions. If there is no difference, the players move on to the next card.

5. *Resolving conflicts.* If there is a difference between the initial positions indicated by the players, they hold a discussion session and try to persuade each other. Either player may ask for another round of secret voting at any time during this discussion. Players may stick to their original positions or shift to new ones. After both have revised their positions, they compare them. The cycle of discussion, revision, and comparison is repeated as often as necessary until players reach consensus.

6. *Scoring the round.* When consensus is achieved, each player compares his or her initial position with the final one and determines the difference. He or she pays the other player the number of poker chips equal to the number of intervals he or she has shifted in his or her position.

7. *Terminating the game.* After reaching consensus on each card, players move on to the next one. The game ends in any one of the following three ways:

- *Mutual success*: If players reach consensus on all cards before they run out of time, the game ends successfully. (This situation is analogous to the completion of the instructional-development project before the deadline.)

- *Pyrrhic success*: If either player runs out of poker chips any time during the game, the game ends in an empty victory for the other player. (This situation is analogous to domination of an instructional-development team by one of the two partners.)

- *Failure*: If players run out of time before all issues cards are discussed, the game ends in a failure. (This situation is analogous to failing to meet the project deadline.)

8. *Determining the winning pair.* The situation simulated in the game does not permit a simple "win-lose" outcome, since individual members of each pair are not competing

against each other. The performance of a pair may be compared with those of other pairs. In this type of scoring, the game leader may use any or all of the following criteria:

 • *Relative status*: A gain of large numbers of chips reflects attempted domination; a loss indicates submission. In the interdependent situation simulated in the game, the ideal is a co-equal status indicated by no difference between the number of chips held by either player at the beginning and at the end of the game. The pair which shows the least difference comes closest to this goal and wins an award on the co-equality criterion.

 • *Open-mindedness*: Co-equal status in the pair could be due to similarity in thinking, acquiescence, or mutual give-and-take. The pair which had the most rounds of revising their positions wins an award on the mutual give-and-take criterion.

 • *Efficiency*: The amount of time spent in resolving interpersonal confrontations is inversely related to the task orientation of the pair. Hence, the pair which took the shortest time to reach consensus on all cards wins an award on the efficiency criterion.

Let us unload the IDIOTS game by removing the instructional-development content. The basic structure of the game is shown in Figure 22 and described below:

1. Divide player groups into pairs.

2. Provide a scenario to each player which describes a confrontation situation.

3. Assign roles and provide different amounts of chips.

4. Players study first conflict issue.

5. Each player takes up a personal position from those offered.

6. Players argue their positions until they reach an agreement on the issue.

7. Players exchange tokens equal to the number of positions they have shifted.

Figure 22

Basic Structure of IDIOTS

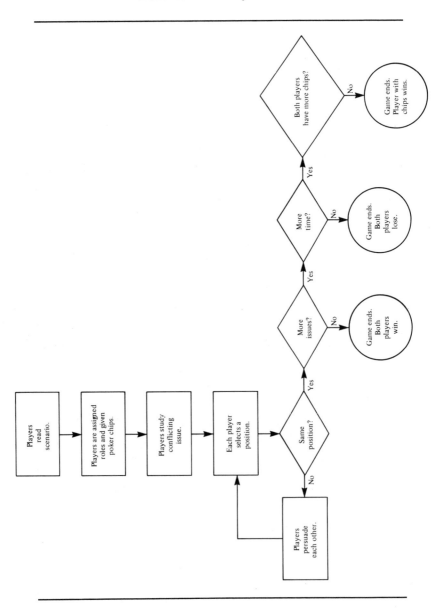

8. Once an issue is resolved, players go on to the next one.

9. Game ends when either all issues have been resolved, time has run out, or one player has run out of chips.

10. There are multiple criteria for determining the winners; these are the basic two:

    (a) within the pair, whoever has accumulated the most chips from the other; and

    (b) among all pairs, the one which has resolved all issues in the shortest period of time.

Adaptation 1. CONFRONTATION

Players: Campus ministers and ombudsmen.

Objective: Resolve conflicts that frequently occur in college and university settings.

Materials:

Poker chips.

A series of issue sheets divided in four as shown in Figure 23.

Number of players: Three. The game is designed for parallel play by many groups of three.

Approximate time requirement: Sixty minutes.

Play of the game:

1. The group arranges itself in a large circle with three chairs placed together at equal intervals around the circle. The number of chairs equals the number of players. (See Figure 24.)

2. One chair in each triad has an "X" symbol. The player in that chair becomes the mediator. The player on his or her right is designated Player A and the one on the left, Player B. Each player receives 20 poker chips.

3. Each mediator divides up the first issue sheet in four. He or she hands each player the appropriate role and keeps the mediator's role.

4. After reading the roles, the mediator shows the position card to both players and asks them to secretly select their positions. He or she then asks them to declare their positions.

5. If the positions differ, players argue, with the mediator intervening. Players must resolve the conflict before five minutes are up.

6. If the issue is resolved (i.e., both players end up on the same position), Players A and B give the mediator one poker chip for each position moved from initial stance. For example, if

Figure 23

Issue Sheet Used in CONFRONTATION

PLAYER A	PLAYER B
You are a teenage undergraduate who has become pregnant. You know who the boy is, but you do not want to marry him anyhow. You have told your mother about your condition but how sorry you are. Your mother and you are meeting the campus minister today to talk about what to do. You are sure about one thing: You want an abortion and you want it now!	You are a white middle-class mother, 40 years old. Your only daughter has become pregnant and confided in you last week. She does not want to marry the boy who got her this way. Worse yet, she wants to have an abortion. You haven't told your husband yet, because he is very strict and short-tempered. You are extremely confused and disturbed as you meet with the campus minister along with your daughter.
MEDIATOR	POSITIONS
You are faced with a mother-daughter confrontation about an unwanted pregnancy. The daughter has told you that she does not want to marry the boy. Nor does she want to have the baby.	1. Immediate, secret abortion. Forget the boy. 2. Tell girl's father. Convince him to agree to abortion and no marriage. 3. Have the baby in secret and put him or her up for adoption. 4. Forget the boy, but have the baby. 5. Marry the boy and have the baby.

Figure 24

Room Arrangement for Playing "CONFRONTATION"

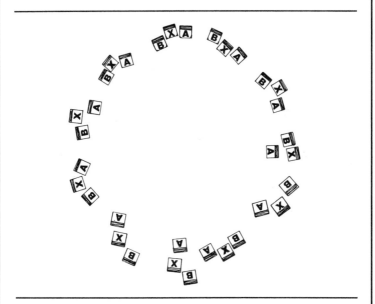

Player A moved from 1 to 4 and Player B from 5 to 4, they would give the mediator 3 and 1 chips, respectively.

If the issue is unresolved, each player in the triad gives up two poker chips to the game leader (i.e., everyone loses when a conflict is unresolved).

7. The game leader signals the next round. All Player A's move to the right and all Player B's move to the left around the circle, the mediators stay in their seats. Thus, new triads are formed. The mediators divide up the second issue sheet and play proceeds as before.

8. Game ends after ten issues. Chips are counted. Among the players (other than the mediator) the one with the most chips wins as the most persuasive player. Among mediators, the one with the most chips wins for having resolved the most divergent conflicts.

9. A debriefing on the principles and problems in conflict resolution follows the play of this simulation game.

Adaptation 2. IT PAYS TO SHARE
Players: Third and fourth grade children.
Objective: Share articles, responsibilities, and rewards through joint decision-making.
Materials:
    A series of conflict stories.
    A flip-chart with a separate sheet for each teacher-told story. On each sheet are five drawings with a brief one-sentence position beside each drawing.
    Picture cards for the character in each story.
    A number wheel for each child.
Number of players: Any regular class.
Approximate time requirement: Ten to 15 minutes for each story.
Play of the game:
    1. The teacher divides the pupils into groups of three, four, or five depending on the story. Each child in the group draws a role card with a picture of the person (or animal) he or she is to be.
    2. The teacher tells a story involving all the characters in a conflict situation where a common decision has to be made. If everyone agrees, everyone wins. If a common decision is not made, everyone loses.
    3. After the brief story, the teacher shows the flip-chart sheet with the possible choices each character can make. He or she asks each pupil to secretly turn his or her number wheel to the position he or she chooses in his or her assigned role.
    4. The groups are now asked to discuss the situation and to come to an agreement within five minutes.
    5. If all agree (as shown by the numbers of the wheels), everyone in the group wins a token plus one token for every group which has not come to an agreement.
    6. The group with the highest number of tokens after all ten stories wins the game.

A Patchwork Quilt

In designing instructional games from frame games, there is one important strategy which is worth emphasizing. We label this as the "patchwork-quilt" approach. Generally speaking, novice game designers tend to follow the basic structure of frame games rather closely and mechanically. This is a good way to get into game design with a relatively high probability of success. However, we should remember that games are composed of many elements and that each of these elements can also be considered as frames.

It is common practice among game designers to adopt the preliminary moves for a game from one source, apply the scoring system from another, plug in the rules from a third, and so on. Frame games have as much to do with an attitude toward game design as they do with design techniques. Every frame game is composed of frame elements making up a pile of patches from which to assemble an endless variety of stimulating instructional activities.

Summary
This chapter on design format deals with the heart of the concept of frame games. Frame games may be analyzed in several ways: in terms of their structure and content and in terms of their rules, roles, scenarios, scoring systems, and media formats. A major part of this chapter focused on designing one's own games using as a base classic or new frame games, simulations or non-simulation frame games. The chapter closed with a reminder that all frame games are made of elements which can be independently transferred and combined to result in a wider variety of innovative instructional activities.

IV.

OUTCOMES

The frame game approach is an effective and efficient way of designing games to help widely divergent learner groups to meet a variety of instructional objectives. This approach offers opportunities to instructors and instructional developers for designing learning materials and methods that accommodate groups of various sizes while still fostering individual learning. Frame games permit us to reap the benefits of instructional games without having to design a game from scratch.

This chapter provides a brief overview of what outcomes can be anticipated from the use of frame games. It also provides some guidelines for conducting games and maintaining a series of delicate balances. It ends with a description of potentially undesirable outcomes and ways to avoid them in using games for instructional purposes.

Frame Games and Instructional Objectives

Frame games facilitate the creation of instructional activities with one or more objectives. Simple SLAPJACK type games focus learner attention on a single discrimination objective in a powerful way. More complex simulation games of the IDIOTS type demand attainment of a whole series of objectives. These games focus on conflict resolution and negotiation skills which require players to:

(a) identify major points of conflict;

(b) classify the type of conflict;

(c) select an appropriate strategy for negotiation; and

(d) resolve the conflict within a given length of time.

These objectives, each of which is complex in itself, may be reached through play of the game. Over and over again, the motivational nature of the activity keeps student attention focused on the objectives. This is an outcome which is characteristic of well-designed instructional games—particularly those based on time-tested frame games.

Because of the intense involvement of games, a highly desirable outcome is that of integration of various skills and knowledge. Most instructional activities are sequential, building from one skill to another. Games generally require simultaneous application of a number of skills and force players to make decisions using several principles and facts at once. Even the simple RUMMY game may make players calculate sums, differences, products, and quotients; classify, group, and build sets; and maintain a game strategy based on probabilities—all at the same time. The integrative nature of games is a unique feature of this instructional design.

Whether the skill is simple sorting or complex decision-making, a game can be created to highlight that skill. The game can also offer an element of reality which is lacking in most structured learning environments. Acquiring information on stock markets is not the same as playing a stock market game. Learning about driving from a manual is not as "real" as playing DRIVING TEST. A desirable outcome of games is the element of realism they provide by allowing players to apply and transfer skills and knowledge to simulated settings. Learners are better prepared to transfer these skills and knowledge to actual application as they exit to reality.

Frame Games and Group Dynamics

One of the most interesting and exciting phenomena we have observed in using frame games is that those who never thought themselves capable of designing a game are delighted to find out that they can. The pleasure of creating a game so motivates the person that when he or she tries the game out with students, it usually works effectively because of the contagious enthusiasm. Once a person has "invented" a game and built its parts, it becomes a personally crafted instructional artifact and it is bound to work! The enthusiasm generated by the teacher or trainer "fires the group" which, in turn, responds with similar enthusiasm.

Most original frame games have been tested and found to succeed; so do their offspring. The games they generate are easily playable and this brings learners rapidly into the game. Because they are playing a game, the classroom atmosphere changes. It is only a game; the learners behave less formally. Despite this, or because of this, there is more intense, involved behaviors being exhibited than in most other learning activities. Time is compressed and appears to fly while the learners are having fun. Players talk to each other easily and freely. Learning shifts away from the teacher and becomes a shared experience among players.

During games, special needs of individual learners can be accommodated through the assignment of appropriate roles to them. The shy, withdrawn child is made important as the judge and the dealer. The slower learner checks the answers from a master list and perhaps learns more than other players. The disruptive person forgets his or her needs for attention in maintaining a record-keeping role. A game, after all, is "only a game." Players can lower their guards and be themselves because everyone knows they are only playing assumed roles.

Frame Games and Group Skills

With the increasing emphasis on individualization, games offer opportunities for learners to acquire interpersonal, interactive skills. To illustrate, the game OUR SCHOOL requires students to mutually plan group activities to improve the school. The time-telling game adapted from SNAKES AND LADDERS puts young children together for learning time-telling skills. Frame games foster group activities that require minimal intervention from the teacher. Mutual learning among players is the result.

The Role of the Instructor in Running Games

Although the teacher (or trainer) is not the central actor after he or she presents an instructional game to learners, he or she nevertheless remains the key person in making it work. There is an art to running games which is a simple process, if one can maintain these seven satisfactory states:

(1) systematic spontaneity;
(2) fixed flexibility;
(3) restless relaxation;
(4) collaborative competition;
(5) interesting instruction;
(6) interpersonal individualization; and
(7) unobtrusive ubiquity.

If you find these states paradoxical, you are only partially correct. Each of these desirable states do contain incompatible elements, but a truly successful game leader is one who can maintain the balance between careful planning and intuitive implementation; decisive judgments and flexible performance; a rapid tempo and a relaxed pace; cooperative interaction and aggressive achievement; a high level of excitement and a patient attention to details; catering to individual needs and providing for group goals; and blending with the background and maintaining a purposeful presence. Here are some tricks of the trade from professional game wardens to provide instructors with a general strategy for using frame games.

Planning carefully and playing it by ear. A noted sage once stated "plan with the left brain and implement with the right." In case there is confusion about which half of the brain is supposed to do what, left-brain planning involves a logical, linear approach and right-brain implementation involves intuitive improvisation. More specifically, here are some suggested guidelines for running games:

1. Allow plenty of time for preparing for the game. Make yourself various checklists and check out the materials, schedules, physical arrangements, and number of players.

2. Go through the game with your friends and become familiar with the sequence. Anticipate emergencies (e.g., only three players turn up, your assistant breaks her leg, or the projector lamp burns out) and brainstorm first-aid activities.

3. Relax when you begin running the game. Even if it turns out to be a bomb, it is still an instructional experience for everyone. Failures provide many insights for debriefing.

4. Just for the fun of it, change the game slightly in the middle of the play. Check for yourself that nothing drastic happens if you play along with the game as you go along.

Declaring a definite "maybe." Begin the game punctually and decisively. But don't become too rigid or ritualistic. Maintain a flexible approach without appearing to be fuzzy or indecisive. Here are some specific suggestions:

1. Introduce the game briefly and describe its rules concisely. Don't lecture about the history and philosophy of gaming. Don't overload your players with esoteric rules and subtle variations. Follow the four-minute rule: If the players are not playing within that time, you are doing superfluous and trivial things.

2. Acknowledge initial confusion on the part of the players and reassure them that they will see the light before it is too late. The best way to learn the game is through

on-the-play training. Remind your players about how they learned to play MONOPOLY.

3. If the players encounter a situation where the rules don't seem to work, make an on-the-spot modification. Feel free to change time limits and score values if you believe that the game can be improved that way.

4. If the players become excessively dependent upon you as the final authority on everything, ease yourself out of the situation. Don't play G.O.D. (Game Overall Director) and become omniscient. When the players ask you a question— "What should we do now?"—turn it back upon them: "What do you want to do?"

Hurrying up and waiting. There is nothing so boring as a slow game in which players and teams wait a long time for their turns. On the other hand, a hectic game may be exciting, but players may miss out on the instructional outcomes at supersonic speeds. Here are some suggestions for maintaining a rapid tempo while providing time for assimilation:

1. Begin the game promptly and get it rolling fast. Announce intermediate time limits and provide information on the remaining time at suitable intervals. Have a big clock on the wall.

2. Time flies when players are having fun. To ensure sufficient time for important activities during later stages of the game and for the debriefing, make yourself a schedule and stick to it. Keep an eye on the clock; appoint a time-keeper, if necessary.

3. Psychological time is more important than the chronological variety. If all teams have finished a specific task ahead of the allotted time, there is no reason to wait out the remaining time. Feel free to "cheat" in your time-keeping whenever necessary.

4. If a player (or a team) has finished a specific task ahead of time, have him or her (or them) revise the product and come

up with an improved version. If a player (or a team) unduly delays the game, provide individual assistance and rush the laggards gently. Very often you may compromise the quantity or quality of a team's performance without major damage to the game experience.

5. If the game gets to be too hectic, slow it down by imposing minimum time requirements. You may introduce bluff-and-challenge rules to force players to pay more attention to each other. You may provide penalties for sloppy or impulsive action.

6. If you feel that the players rushed through the game and ignored its instructional message, replay the same game. This is especially suitable for non-simulation games of short duration.

Avoiding cut-throat competition and indifferent interaction. Competition is neither good nor bad, but is a fact of life. You need some competition to motivate players but not so much that winning the game becomes the only aim and their obsession with score points clouds their perception of the main points. The other extreme of total de-emphasis of all competition results in reduced distraction but increased boredom. Guidelines for maintaining an optimum level of cooperation-competition include the following:

1. Let the scores speak for themselves at the end of the game. Players know who won and who lost without your dwelling upon the agony of defeat.

2. Recognize and reinforce hard work and smart strategy, but do so in a criterion-based fashion. Avoid making unnecessary comparisons among different players and teams.

3. You can change the rules to reduce conflict among players and increase conflict between players and constraints (e.g., time limits) and standards (e.g., previous records).

4. Increase the number of ways in which players win so that more players have the opportunity. It is much more realistic to have multiple criteria for winning a game than to

have a single criterion. Speed, quantity, quality, efficiency, fluency, and creativity are some of the dimensions of winning which may be applied to the same game.

5. Set up different criteria for different players. For example, the criteria for the prosecutor may differ from those for the defendant and from those for the jurors. Better yet, allow each person to publicly or privately specify his or her own criteria and try to achieve them.

Ensuring intrinsic excitement. You need the game to get the horse to water, but if you keep up the excitement of play, the horse may not drink anything. An ideal game provides the optimum amount of motivation so that learning is facilitated rather than hampered. Since there are very few ideal games around, here are some tips for keeping the interest-instruction dimension in balance:

1. Check the relationship between the instructional objectives and the scoring system of the game. If they are not directly correlated, make suitable adjustments so that winning the game reflects the attainment of the objectives.

2. Watch out for the chance elements in the game. If they do not match real-life probabilities, you could have a major problem.

3. If you feel that the players are getting too excited about the game and neglecting its instructional objectives, call a time out and discuss the situation with the players. Conduct a "mini-debriefing" in the middle of the game so that major instructional messages are not lost.

4. If the game becomes too dull and didactic, spice it up with bonus scores, bluff-and-challenge rules, increased chance elements, and a faster pace.

5. Have a series of structured questions to highlight the instructional content during debriefing. Maximize learning outcomes through appropriate follow-up assignments that require an application of the skills and knowledge gained from the game.

Wholesale individualization. Games can contribute significantly to individualized learning, if you attend to the strengths and weaknesses of each player. Of course, this does not mean that you should pander to the wants of an individual at the expense of the needs of the group. Here are some useful suggestions for personalizing the play process:

1. In individual games, make sure that the players are evenly matched; there is nothing so demoralizing as consistently losing and nothing so ineffective as constantly winning. If there is too much of an imbalance among players, use appropriate handicaps: The weaker player may use three dice instead of two, receive extra cards, and take his or her turn more frequently.

2. In team games, try to achieve as much imbalance within each team as possible. This ensures that team members mutually teach and learn.

3. Identify bashful players and assign them special roles (e.g., judge) to encourage their active participation. Identify show-offs and smart alecks and assign them appropriate roles (e.g., score-keeper) to channel their excess energy into constructive activities. In any group, there are always a few people who are too timid or too aggressive to play the game. Do not encourage the latter or intimidate the former. In extreme cases, take them off the game and give them some meaningful assignment to assist you in running the game.

4. Identify those players who show special talent for the game strategy or its instructional content. Conduct special, individual debriefings with each of these players and assign them the follow-up task of modifying and improving the game.

Participating discreetly. During the game session, there are periods when you should be self-effacing and let the game flow by itself. And then there are times when you need to be assertive and get everyone's attention. Here are some suggestions for achieving this schizophrenic role:

1. The hardest job in running a game is keeping out of the way. Here are some ways to keep yourself out of mischief when the players are having fun: (1) covertly anticipate strategies of different players and (2) plan for changes in the next run of the same game.

2. With a small number of players and with certain types of games, you, too, may participate in the actual play. If you do, make sure that you are not withholding any vital information or attempting to dominate the play.

3. Another useful activity during the play of the game is to go around and carefully observe players' action. Record insightful incidents and creative comments for use during the debriefing.

4. When you have to make an important announcement (e.g., new rules or rule changes), make sure that everyone is listening. One way to ensure this is to go to each team and talk to its members.

5. When there is an important announcement to be made and players are intensely involved in the game, you may try turning off the lights briefly.

6. Another good way to get across important messages is to put them on a transparency and project them on a screen. You have to inform your players of this arrangement at the beginning of the session. Used sparingly and interspersed with bonus announcements (e.g., "First player to tag the game leader gets 20 extra points"), this technique works wonders.

Different strokes for different folks. These suggestions are neither comprehensive nor mutually exclusive. They work for some, but you will have to try them out for yourself and modify them to suit your style.

There is no substitute for actual experience in acquiring a personal, professional game-running style. While the specific suggestions given above may or may not work for you, the basic concept of a balancing act and a trade-off among different variables should provide you some guidelines with which to begin.

Undesirable Outcomes (and How to Avoid Them)

Not all game outcomes are likely to be positive ones. Here are some negative results that can occur and some suggestions on how you might avoid them in your own games:

1. Non-competitors can be damaged. Games have some element of conflict built into them, and if this conflict resolves itself into highly aggressive competition, the non-assertive type can become excluded and sometimes even destroyed. Build in special roles for such persons. Direct conflict away from interplayer competition. Reward cooperation. Team up the assertive ones with the meek.

2. With the emphasis on the group interaction, individuals can get lost. The major advantage of games—group learning—can become a disadvantage when individuals get clobbered during decision-making activities or pushed aside because of poor game skills. Even the simple frame games reward the better game players. Build into the game chance factors for slower learners. Make sure that discussion rules provide equal time for each player. Judging, score-keeping, dealing cards, and even making game parts can be assigned to individuals to help each gain the most from your game.

3. Once wound up, a group is hard to wind down. Games are so motivating that they may stir up hornets' nests with unpleasant consequences. Who wants to listen to a boring lecture after an exciting game? And when can we play again? Schedule game activities close to natural break periods (e.g., lunch or end of the day). Build in logical follow-up activities that maximize learning from the game. Get players to suggest ways in which what they learned from the game can be applied to real life. Have them follow their own suggestions.

4. A lot of precious time is burnt up in achieving very few instructional objectives. A game takes time to prepare and play. It sometimes takes up an inordinate amount of time in an already tight schedule. Is the game really worth the candle? The best way to avoid wasting time is to select

high-priority objectives that are not being efficiently attained by other instructional design formats. If students or trainees are already doing well in some part of a course, why tamper? The highest pay-off for a big game-design investment is where the need is greatest. If the game succeeds, the time and effort can be more easily justified.

5. In the heat of gaming, undesirable notions can be acquired. This is best illustrated by an anecdote. We received a game about life in a totalitarian state designed for elementary school children. We had our sons play the game. It was fun. At the end of the game, we asked Raja "What did you learn from the game?" His reply, "It is better to denounce your mother than your father. You get more points." Robbie, a little younger, heartily agreed. Players' defenses are down during a game, and care must be taken in designing your game to avoid prejudicial information, inaccuracies, or misleading conclusions. Games are powerful vehicles for helping learners acquire skills, knowledge, and attitudes—of the undesirable variety just as readily as the desirable ones.

6. Monitoring learning during a game is a nightmare. If you have the urge to grade every learning activity, games pose problems. Too many factors interact in a game to keep track of them completely. Nevertheless, there are some ways for monitoring learning during a game:

- Observe play. Are the players following the rules with ease?
- Listen and note down comments you overhear from players. Do they reflect what you designed your game for?
- Stop and ask brief questions of players as they wait their turns. How appropriately do they reply?
- Focus on an individual player for two minutes. What is he or she doing?
- Test learners before and after the game. Are there any gains?

Summary

This chapter focused on the outcomes of the application of frame games. In a broader sense, it also dealt with learning outcomes from the use of instructional games in general. Frame games help designers produce instructional games rapidly without learning a whole new set of skills. The games they produce help learners attain instructional objectives in a highly motivating way. The games alter the group dynamics of normal classroom settings in a positive direction. Mutual learning through increased learner participation results. Group interaction skills are highlighted.

Although games direct attention away from the teacher or trainer, he or she nevertheless plays a key role in making the game work optimally by maintaining a delicate balance between authoritarianism and laissez-faire, keeping activities spontaneous and at the same time on target. Games can result in a number of negative outcomes, if some special precautions are not taken.

V.

DEVELOPMENTAL GUIDE

This final chapter provides a brief developmental guide for designing your own games from frame games. The Design Format chapter presented a smorgasbord containing a considerable number of potential frames from which to build your own games. We refer you back to this chapter when you are ready to actually get into design. But before doing that, we would like to outline the major steps in the design process. We have added extra details on the evaluation of games toward the end because we believe very strongly in testing our products with representative learners and revising them on the basis of their reactions, remarks, and responses. It is our firm contention that a good thing can always be made better.

1. Specifying the purpose of your game. Before designing a game, begin by asking yourself, "What is the overall purpose of the game to be?" and, "What must my learners come away with?" Once you have made a comprehensive statement of the purpose of the game, break it down into a set of instructional objectives. Write your purpose and objectives from the learners' (and not your own) point of view. Focus on your learners right from the start.

2. Specifying the key elements to be incorporated into the game. What elements, persons, institutions, symbols, etc., must be included in your game? Make an exhaustive list and omit any elements later. Determine the relationships between the elements. How do they all fit together? A diagram or verbal description helps here. If this step is omitted, you may end up with inaccuracies or misleading relationships as a result of playing your game.

3. Selecting a frame. Survey existing frames. You should avidly collect all types of games, since each one is a potential frame game. Choose a frame game which best fits your objectives and players. Several may do, but one usually comes through most saliently. Pick apart the frame. Isolate the major elements. Remember, a frame game is like a standard housing blueprint. It needs tailoring and modification before you start building.

4. Specifying adaptations. Here you begin to load your content onto the selected frame. Specify your rules and the play of the game. Describe the roles for each player. Write a scenario to give an appropriate storyline to the game. Design the scoring system. Use the one from the original frame game, but modify it suitably. Or, select the scoring system from another game, if it will better suit the instructional objectives.

5. Producing the adapted game. Physically create (or have your learners create) the game components. Some of these can be borrowed from other games (e.g., dice, spinners, tokens, poker chips, timers, and game boards). Produce a clear set of rules to which players can refer. If possible, flowchart the play of the game for your reference. Package the game. Put all the parts together in a suitable (and attractive) container. Clear plastic zip-lock bags or recovered puzzle boxes make suitable containers.

6. Evaluating and revising your game. To make your game playable and instructional, continuously evaluate and modify it. Here is a chronology of evaluation activities:

Stage I. Game Designer Self-Evaluation

After preparing your first crude design, examine it yourself critically. Ask yourself the following questions:

- Are the rules of the game clearly related to its instructional objectives?
- Does winning the game depend on attainment of the game objectives?
- Can game materials be easily handled by the players?
- Is the scoring system clear?
- Does the game have the right combination of chance and skill for the level of the players and the type of objectives?
- Am I building any undesirable biases into the game?

Stage II. Expert Appraisal

Submit the game, its objectives, and explanatory materials to such experts as other game designers, subject-matter specialists, and instructors, as soon as they are in some comprehensible form. Prepare a checklist and an interview questionnaire to collect systematic feedback from these experts. Permit the experts to make their own free comments and suggestions for revisions.

Stage III. Limited Local Tryout

Round up a group of available people to play the game. If these players are different from the ultimate player population, have them role-play. Observe the players as they play. Take notes during the game on its weaknesses and problems. Make on-the-spot changes, if necessary. Try out alternate rules on scoring systems. Interfere as little as possible in the play of the game. After the game, encourage players to express their confusions and frustrations. Revise and clean up the game based on player feedback.

Stage IV. Game Tryout with Representative Players

Select a few representative players and a naturalistic setting. Administer pretests, if necessary. Present the game with its rules in its "final" form. Collect data on how the game proceeds without any interference on your part. Administer posttests, if necessary. Elicit comments and suggestions from the players. Make suitable revisions and prepare the game for testing in your absence.

Stage V. Hands-Off Testing

Turn the game entirely over to someone else to run. Prepare all necessary game materials and test instruments. Keep away from the trial, as it should take place in a natural setting. Listen in during the postgame debriefing. Ask the game runner for his or her comments and suggestions. Fine tune as a result of this evaluation.

Stage VI. Long-Term Evaluation

Periodically monitor the game after it has been launched. Follow up its use to see if the content is still relevant and accurate and if the game is still meeting its objectives. Update the game as necessary or withdraw it if it no longer serves any useful purpose.

Summary

This final chapter provided a brief step-by-step plan for designing your own games from frame games. It has particularly emphasized the all-too-frequently neglected areas of evaluation and revision.

Teachers, trainers, and instructional developers are all busy people and perhaps it is asking too much to carefully test everything they produce. But the frame game approach to game design cuts down on the time required to produce a good game. Invest a little of this time back into careful evaluation and revision of your product. We promise that it will pay off.

But enough talk. We are getting restless. Let's play a game—your game!

VI.

RESOURCES

BOOKS WITH USABLE FRAMES

Diagram Group. *The Way to Play.* New York: Paddington Press Ltd., 1975.

While almost any paperback *Hoyle's* will provide you with a wealth of information on any of the time-tested classic games, this book is our favorite. It describes hundreds of games from all around the world. You should be able to derive many of the frames and use them for instructional purposes.

Pfeiffer, J.W., and Jones, J.E. *A Handbook of Structured Experiences for Human Relations Training.* La Jolla, California: University Associates, 1976.

"Structured experiences" are content-free frames originally intended to demonstrate various aspects of human relations. You may find many of these frames suitable for loading different instructional content. This is a series which has six volumes (according to our last count) and annual updates.

Sackson, S. *A Gamut of Games.* New York: Castle Books, 1969.

Sid Sackson is perhaps the most diabolically clever modern game designer. This book contains a number of unusual games with innovative frames.

BOOKS ON GAMES

Carney, T.F. *No Limits to Growth.* Winnipeg, Canada: Harbeck and Associates Ltd., 1976.
This book deals with a number of "mind expanding techniques" including an interesting introduction to frame games.

DeVries, D.L., and Associates. *Teams-Games-Tournament: The Team Learning Process.* Englewood Cliffs, New Jersey: Educational Technology Publications, 1980.

Thiagarajan, S., and Stolovitch, H.D. *Instructional Simulation Games.* Englewood Cliffs, New Jersey: Educational Technology Publications, 1978.
These two books in the Instructional Design Library series deal with related topics.

DIRECTORIES

Horn, R. *The Guide to Simulations/Games for Education and Training.* Cranford, New Jersey: Didactic Systems, 1976.
Contains classified listings and comprehensive descriptions of more than 1400 simulations and games for all subject matters and educational levels. Has a special section on frame games.

Stadsklev, R. *Handbook of Simulation Gaming in Social Education.* University, Alabama: University of Alabama, 1975.
Contains comprehensive listings and detailed reviews of hundreds of simulations and games in the broad area of social sciences. The first part is a textbook on the design and use of games.

JOURNALS

Simulation and Games. An interdisciplinary, scholarly quarterly published by SAGE Publications (275 S. Beverly Drive, Beverly Hills, California 90212).

Journal of Experiential Learning and Simulation. Another quarterly journal with an emphasis on business education, published by Elsevier North Holland (52 Vanderbilt Avenue, New York, New York 10017).

PROFESSIONAL ASSOCIATION
North American Simulation and Gaming Association (c/o COMEX, Davidson Conference Center, University of Southern California, University Park, Los Angeles, California 90007).
The leading professional society for serious gamesters. Conducts an annual conference in different parts of the country.

WORKSHOPS
The Games Preserve (R.D. 1355, Fleetwood, Pennsylvania 19522; Telephone: (215) 987-3456). This play-study environment is housed in a renovated barn on 25 acres of open fields and woods. The area includes a fabulous collection of games and an extensive library of books related to the study of play from anthropological, sociological, and psychological approaches. Bernie DeKoven (author of *The Well-Played Game,* contributing editor to *Games* magazine, and former director of the New Games Foundation) conducts workshops on play education.

The University of Michigan Extension Gaming Service (350 South Thayer Street, Ann Arbor, Michigan 48109; Telephone: (313) 763-1010). University of Michigan at Ann Arbor has been the headquarters for frame games for many years. The Extension Gaming Service conducts excellent workshops on playing, conducting, and building games.

Instructional Alternatives (4423 East Trailridge Road, Bloomington, Indiana 47401; Telephone: (812) 336-1551). The authors of the book and Dr. Diane Dormant conduct a

number of different on-site workshops on the use of frame
games for effective training, productive meetings, and efficient evaluation. These custom-tailored, competency-based
workshops deal with the selection and evaluation of commercial frame games, design of local adaptations, and the use of
frame games.

HAROLD D. STOLOVITCH has taught children and adults in a number of different settings and cultures for more than 15 years. A fluent speaker of English and French, he has conducted extremely successful courses and workshops in various parts of Africa, the United States, and Canada. He is the designer of a number of games and author of articles on simulations/games as well as various aspects of instructional development and evaluation. He is currently at the Universite de Montreal, where he teaches courses and directs research on instructional technology. He is also associate dean for research of the education faculty. Stolovitch has taught graduate courses on the design, evaluation, and use of simulations/games in the U.S. and Canada.

SIVASAILAM ("Thiagi") THIAGARAJAN began his career in education in Madras, India, where he taught high school physics and math for six years. His home-grown instructional innovations attracted the attention of Dr. Douglas Ellson, who invited him to come to the United States and work for him. Thiagarajan received his Ph.D. in Instructional Systems Technology from Indiana University. His professional experiences in the United States include administering six major instructional developmental projects, consulting with 40 organizations, serving on the editorial board of six professional journals, participating in national and international advisory panels, and conducting more than 100 workshops all over the country. He has published 12 books and more than 100 articles on different aspects of instructional and performance technology, and has produced 30 audiovisual training modules and 15 simulations/games.